highways to

JOBS

for women

HOW TO PICK COLLEGE COURSES FOR YOUR CAREER

Josephine H. Gerth

New York

THE WOMAN'S PRESS

IN COLLEGE you will learn many facts, develop a number of abilities and, when you become the proud possessor of your Bachelor's degree, you should have the potentialities to become a well-integrated personality with a purpose and place in the world. You will not become such an individual, however, merely by sojourning for four years on a college campus. That is why this book will be invaluable to you, if you read it carefully and use it diligently as a workbook, beginning with your freshman year. *Highways to Jobs for Women* is unique in its emphasis and method of presentation. Stress is placed on your initiative, your study of job titles, the requirements of the job and the part that personality plays in the choice of a vocation, as well as in the success and happiness in the chosen work.

The author approaches the place of the liberal arts college in training students for vocations from an unusual, and to my way of thinking, realistically sensible viewpoint. A liberal arts college is not vocational—is prevocational or general at best— yet every one of its students will want some special "world of work," in which to participate. Even the girl who marries and devotes most of her time to a home and children, needs and should have outside activities in which she has a deep, vigorous interest.

Except in the strictly professional fields, or in the area of jobs requiring special skills, vocations are open to the person trained to think straight, to find out about the things she does not know and how to do them. A large number of graduates drift by some chance, fortunate or otherwise, into jobs which seem to have a remote connection with their major in college. But on the job, they discover previously unrealized interests and abilities; they find themselves more capable and creative than they had imagined themselves to be.

It is also important to emphasize the competitiveness of the world in which we now live. None of us can be overprepared if we are to find a place for ourselves and to make an effective contribution. The relationship of the liberal arts college to those two necessities has been widely discussed, because of the thinking and planning which are mandatory if its great variety of subjects and interests is to be channelled toward a particular goal. All this, however, can be used to advantage by the student who recognizes both the infinite job possibilities to which a well-planned liberal arts curriculum can lead and the personal maturity that it can develop.

The plan of vocational exploration presented here seems, at first glance, to require all of your time. Certainly it does put all the responsibility upon you, but once having accepted that fact you will find help at every hand—the dean's office, for example, or your adviser. When scientifically validated tests can reveal answers to your problem, counselors will suggest these aids. That's an ideal setup, isn't it? But by now you have learned that ideal setups usually leave you where you started. So, off the record, from dean to student, may I say, "Depend upon yourself, ask for help in the accustomed channels, but count only on yourself."

Ann Anthony

DEAN OF STUDENTS,
HUNTER COLLEGE OF THE CITY OF NEW YORK

TABLE OF CONTENTS

HIGHWAYS TO JOBS FOR WOMEN

"BISHOP BLOUGRAM'S APOLOGY"

The common problem, yours, mine, everyone's,

Is—not to fancy what were fair in life

Provided it could be, but, finding first

What may be, then how to make it fair,

Up to our means: a very different thing!

No abstract, intellectual plan of life

Quite irrespective of life's plainest laws,

But one, a man, who is man and nothing more

May lead within a world which (by your leave)

Is Rome or London, not Fool's-paradise

Embellish Rome, idealize away,

Make paradise of London if you can

You're welcome, nay, you're wise.

ROBERT BROWNING

1
YOU AND COLLEGE

All men are specialists at last, but there is a time for choice and it is not the time of youth. Youth wants to be all things at once and should be given a go at it. When the experiment is done, a specialty will announce itself. Meanwhile there is not the hurry we suppose there is—and so supposing, threaten our society with a caste system of predestined trades and professions such as a democracy may find it difficult to survive.

—MARK VAN DOREN[1]

THIS IS A VOCATIONAL GUIDANCE WORKBOOK. Half of it is written for you. The second half you will write yourself, because vocational guidance must have your participation. There are thousands of college women, and a great deal is known about their vocational wishes and abilities. A great deal is known also about jobs for them. The part written for you, therefore, concerns two things: *you*, as a college woman, and *jobs*, as they exist today. The part personally contributed concerns you—a unique individual, about whom no one knows—and jobs as they will exist for you tomorrow. This book asks you to do for yourself in particular what has been done for college graduates in general, and in the matching process to find an occupational self—a special world of work. Try it and see! In the following chapters you will begin to search with diligence for that important goal, which is the work you will enjoy doing after college.

"Oh, I'll do anything that pays five thousand dollars a day, for a start," says one girl. She is meeting the vocational worry with a joke.

[1]From *Liberal Education,* by Mark Van Doren. Reproduced by permission of Henry Holt and Company, Inc. Copyright, 1943, by Mark Van Doren.

1

Another says, "My father knows the president of every company. . . ." She offers bravado to kill doubt.

A third girl volunteers, "Oh, don't worry about what you'll do after college; something will turn up, it always does." Worry here is drugged with nonchalance.

But another girl has the solution. "I know what I'm going to do after college—I'm going to get married, and end it all." End all the doubts? For a time.

These are obviously painkillers, sedatives. Why not accept the challenge yourself? It concerns you, not your family, friends or husband. Suppose father's influence is extensive. Suppose there really are wealthy suitors on the doorstep. That is wonderful. Friends envy you. But aren't you curious, just a little, about what pay roll title you can fill successfully?

you know MORE than you think you do

Many students have gone through college and emerged none the wiser about their abilities than when they entered. The saddest thing a counselor hears comes from the student who says after graduation, "I really haven't the slightest idea how I want to earn a living."

Even this perplexed graduate knows more than she thinks she knows. Her problem seems unsolvable only because she is trying to unravel it in a minute. You are not going to wait until graduation day or until you have to face a prospective employer before finding out what you want to do to earn a living. Begin the search *now*—in Chapter II. It will not be completed in one day, but it will be completed by graduation time if you have the courage to start before fate forces you to learn by blundering. Insights about yourself and your occupational abilities will develop as you go through college. These are too precious—and amusing—to be forgotten. They will evaporate unless you seize them as they appear, good, bad, indifferent though they may be. Watch them grow. Time, and you, growing in maturity, will evaluate them. These flashes are all you. You thought them up so they are to be respected. See the pattern these ideas make. All that concerns you will help in discovering yourself.

you know LESS than you think you do

When you enter college, the world is a neat little circle, comprised of family, friends, community. Possibly you may know about the occupations represented in that small sphere. The probabilities are that you know only the high points of these jobs, only about the few people who have obtained distinction, perhaps publicity, through their occupations. You do not know the steps which lead to jobs in the larger circumference. Certainly you do not yet realize the exciting new world of work which the alchemy of your presence will make. Your individual contribution will make that change, and what you don't know about that undiscovered continent, no one else knows either.

The world, however, is certainly not waiting for anyone to come bouncing out of college saying, "They told me I was needed; here I am, what's the salary?" No one wants that. Humanity, however, is desperately waiting for you right this minute, before finishing college, to get down to the serious business of finding out what its needs are and how you may serve them, very specifically. You did not make the problems and sorrows of the world, but you must discover how to help solve them. The discovery will be new, because you are new. This discovery will be a day-by-day uncovering.

go to college? what for?

Since college is concerned with courses—majors and minors—not with job titles and self-analysis, you say, "Don't I need to know what I want to do in order to choose the right courses for job preparation? In fact, I'm going to college in order to get a job."

There is no measuring stick by which anyone may appraise the value of a college education; but your family, neighbors and friends, as well as you, somehow regard college as preparation for a career—a definite occupation which has a pay roll title and a pay roll return. Consequently, your questions, quite naturally, are, "What do I want to study in college? What do I want to do?" These are haunting questions which

can make one feel like the newly elected May queen who was
having difficulty remembering appointments. It was time
for a rehearsal here, an appointment with the dressmaker
there. Run, run, run. Looking like the queen of the witches,
she burst in upon her roommate demanding, "Ought I to be
anywhere?"

Each girl who goes to college certainly can list a dozen reasons. Here we are concerned with those relating to vocations.
Right now that vocation is couched in vague terms such as
these: "I want a job where I can meet people," "I want to do
something different," "I want to travel abroad." Vague terms
expressing real feelings. During the first two undergraduate
years, you should certainly be permitted to express vocational
aims in these "feeling" terms. Later, in Chapters IV and V,
these ideas must be stated in the cold job specification language which the employer understands. But for the time
being, you may say, vocationally speaking, that you are going
to college to prepare for "the career you really want," even
though you do not know its title. The serious business of
making choices is now your concern.

In some localities choices are made easily. A tourist on a
country walking trip employed a schoolboy as a guide. The
guide thought many things the traveler did were strange, but
particularly amusing was the stranger's habit of frequently
looking at his watch.

"Why do you look at your watch?" the youngster finally
asked.

"Why," replied the traveler, "the watch tells me when I
should rest, when I should eat, and how fast to walk."

"Oh," replied the boy, "why don't you throw away your
watch and do as you please?"

The formula of the young boy is too simple. In our society,
we just can't throw away our watches. We are bound inex-
tricably in a maze, as ponderous as the German combination
Widerwillige Zeitgebundenheit: bound unwillingly to time.
Only in our dreams are we released from those bonds. Even
the satisfactions obtained from day-to-day living are determined
by ultimate objectives. We are not sure, quite naturally, what

these objectives are, but if we purposefully allow it to, the liberal arts college can disclose them.

You would like particularly to be sure of your "satisfactions" and your "ultimate objectives" when the time comes to choose elective studies in the college curriculum. It may be a simple matter to keep vocational questions in your subconscious mind while following courses which are listed under the heading, "Required of All Students." But once you are free to choose, then vocational questions push for an answer. Without encouraging you to throw away your watch, we most emphatically do urge you to do as you please in those areas where the college authorities give opportunity for choice. The high school counselor recognized this when he wisely countered a student's challenge, "Well, if I do go to college, I'll go just to have a good time!" with the reply, "There's no better place to have it."

Here we may use such flippant terms as "do as you please" and "have a good time," because in Chapters III, IV and V we shall show that you are obliged to do so. The college counselor often would like to say to girls choosing their electives, what the young mother said to her nine-year-old son whom she was forcing to attend a girl's party, "You have a good time or I'll spank you!"

how wonderful

So all one needs to do is go to college for a good time, pick out courses, choose majors according to their entertainment value, concentrate on self-analysis, and lo, one's lifework becomes apparent. You would hate it, if that could be done so easily. All that has been said and all that follows, the part that is written and the part you are asked to write, have been predicated upon the assumption that you will dig seriously to find out who and what you are, what your mind enjoys doing, what your feelings are about studies and about employment. Having finished high school, you are at least accustomed to the fact that often the work of the world is done by weary people, and that all ideal situations have their decidedly unideal aspects. You are growing up, but still there is the all-pervading truth that you have likes and dislikes. This workbook dares you to discover what they are and how they can be made to serve both your needs and those of the world.

Here is urged a dangerous philosophy; the risks are high, compelling. In the long run, you will do, or keep trying to do, what is in your nature; in other words, you will do what pleases you, and college provides the time, place and opportunity to find out what that is. It also has its own ration of grind, routine and boredom. Those necessities are part of any and every duty. A five-year-old child cannot tolerate these facts of life. How far away from the five-year-old child are you?

To seek advice and encouragement for every decision that must be made, for every step that must be taken, is as serious a mistake as to refuse any assistance. You know some help-seekers. You call them "soft," "infantile." So does the college adviser and the employer. Are you soft? If so, you might possibly read through this manual, but you certainly will find too many obstacles ever to do a whit of the work suggested here. You may, however, be in the second, the no-help-ever group. "I'll show them how smart I am" might be their motto. You are not "soft"—but "hard." Without mentioning any of the many causes for such behavior patterns, we are safe in saying that you, too, will excuse yourself from trying to solve personal vocational problems by forethought. You will prefer trusting to luck.

Let us assume you have an even balance, are willing to do all the work, but will stop, look and listen along the way and ask for help, take it and use it, with genuine appreciation and full responsibility. The danger, the lure and excitement offered by the liberal arts curriculum are here because one never exhausts its possibilities. Sciences, humanities, social sciences—you can do anything you want with them.

At the start of this journey of self-discovery, your vocational thoughts may be arrogantly pretentious, utterly impossible. If you really are entertaining such vagaries, put them down, acknowledge their existence and expose them to the test of reality. How else can adolescent ideas grow into maturity? Ideas can be either expressed or repressed. This vocational diary offers the security of oblivion and dares you to write down your "wild ideas" and then seriously to check their validity. Thoreau said, "If you have built castles in the air, your work need not be lost; that is where they should be. Now put the foundations under them."

Last year's graduating class may seem too old to be allowed to live. You will gaze at alumnae returning to the campus for their first or second class reunion and think, "Why do they ever bother? They're so old!" You'll get there yourself so soon. Do you want to spend one or two whole years just playing around hit-and-miss? Like a quick breath, one and two years slip into five and ten, and then fate is forcing you to learn about yourself by blundering. Vocational aptitude tests may help. But even the most enthusiastic exponents of vocational analysis by tests admit that the vocational potentiality of every individual is so varied that tests are weak helpers. Nor are there tests, as yet, which predict ability to grow, or measure degrees of ambition. Whether you decide to take a battery of them and trust their "results," whether you decide to trust all to the advice of parents, friends or any outside authority— the *responsibility* for the choice still remains with you.

"My father wants me to . . ."

"My friends say I'd be good at . . ."

"The tests say I'd do well as a . . ."

However you vary the above remarks, the interpretation of these recommendations is yours. Those who wish to evade this responsibility, who consciously or unconsciously want some outside authority to make decisions for them, will blunder about until they finally accept the responsibility which has always been theirs. Sometimes, people don't live that long!

Conspicuous by its absence from this book is pressure sales talk in behalf of a particular profession or field of work. All aspects of welfare, religious and service occupations, for example, are burdened with workers who have been drawn into these fields by emotional appeals, without thorough self-knowledge. Service vocations receive the greatest criticism, but this is just as true of certain business careers whose supposed glamour attracts the unequipped.

From here on you will need a pencil—and perhaps a lock and key. Many times you will wish to discuss discoveries and decisions with a college adviser or dean. They will welcome the evidence of definite thought taken in solving a personal problem. You will go to the conference, not as a recipient of relief, but as the active agent—the director of exploration. Sometimes you will feel like working in Chapter III, sometimes in other chapters. Obviously you may skip around, after a first glance at the whole, and skip around you should. Such a varied procedure, however, is not possible in presentation. That must be done in an orderly fashion.

In general you will be doing five things, some at one time, some at another, or, perhaps, doing several things at once:

1. You will approach the vocational mystery by seeking to find out who you are, and what in the liberal arts curriculum interests you most. (Chapter II)
2. All the while you will be observing and recording the names of occupations. You can easily find one a day you have never dreamed existed. (Chapter III)
3. You will seek, discover and record the specific skill requirements of these newly found occupational titles. (Chapters IV and V)
4. You will observe, discover and record your own abilities. (Chapter VI)
5. You will match occupational titles to these abilities.

For generations students have thought that "What shall I study at college?" depended upon "What I want to do after college." But generations of graduates whose careers have been delayed by frustration and floundering know that what you do at college and what you do subsequently depend upon the connecting agent between school and work. That liaison agent is you. To know yourself is a harder task than to know any other objective thing. To learn occupational titles and skill specifications is easy by comparison. Chapters III, IV and V present the easier task; Chapters II and VI the harder, in that they ask you to write about that unknown quantity, you!

2

MOSTLY ABOUT YOU

I give you the universe new and unhandled every hour. You think in your idle hours that there is literature, history, science behind you so accumulated as to exhaust thought and prescribe your own future and the future. In your sane moments you shall see that not a line has yet been written, that for all the poetry there is in the world, your first sensation on entering a wood or standing on the shore of a lake has not been chanted yet. It remains for you, so does all thought, all object, all life remain unwritten still.

—RALPH WALDO EMERSON, *Journals*—1838

WHAT KIND OF PERSON ARE YOU? To find answers to that question you might take numerous tests which purport to describe personality. Of course, you have some ideas concerning your likes and dislikes. Your friends and family also can add information. You may not agree with any of their descriptions, or may even feel that they actually don't know anything about the real you. For example, you certainly have heard your mother say, "She's a studious girl" (or the opposite). Friends may have labelled you "a good mixer," or as a person who does everything with skill. As one personnel director has commented, "Some portion of every girl's life is devoted to looking in the mirror, not so much from vanity, as to decide what she can do about what she sees."

All these methods of knowing yourself look inward. The liberal arts curriculum, however, offers another method, that of losing yourself in its studies, of turning your mind from introspection to finding in this infinite, your own true personality. Here is the greatest adventure any curriculum could offer.

Suppose you choose to study a foreign language, German, for example, and come across this simple sentence (every student of German reads these Heath books):

Vom Augsburger Religionsfrieden an bis zum Ausbruch des dreissigjährigen Krieges ist eine der längsten Friedenszeiten der deutschen Geschichte.

From the Peace of Augsburg [which granted religious freedom, 1555] to the outbreak of the Thirty Years War [1648], is one of the longest times of peace in German history.[1]

Like a dull weight, the pathos of that statement strikes you. It is not merely a statement; it becomes an exclamation of wonder. You ask whether such constant strife is the history of other nations. If so, how has civilization progressed? What explains all the beauty which has developed in these constantly warring countries? You begin to think of the creative uses of sorrow and struggle, of the perversion of human emotions, which brought about all this conflict. You might even relate these national traits to individuals. These thoughts acquaint you with the facts of history to be sure, but they also tell you something about yourself: In the first place, you would like to know more about history; in the second, you are becoming somewhat of a philosopher; or maybe it is psychology that beckons.

The fact that two plus two equals four might not seem exciting until you take a course in statistics. Here you find out how to select a sample of a large population so that the sample will be a valid representation of the characteristics of the whole population! If you respond to this, you are learning more than statistics: You are discovering that you have a logical mind that enjoys logical exercises and can think in abstract terms; you are glimpsing a universe of law.

the thrill's the thing

Colleges offering electives require a common base upon which the major choice is made. From that base you may have, here and there, flashes of light, a thrill which will open new vistas of learning. This is a private signal for further specialization.

---

[1] Kaufmann, Friedrich Wilhelm, and Balduf, Emery W., *Inductive Readings in German, Book III.* D. C. Heath, Chicago, 1929, p. 57.

Dr. Robert M. Hutchins, chancellor of the University of
Chicago, might call this the "chiropractic approach" to educational guidance, which would require an "X-ray examination
of the vertebrae"[2] to make its presence known in a more practical manner. You know, however, when your mind has been
stimulated, your spirit enlivened by facts which to others in
the class, and maybe to the teacher, have appeared as ordinary
comments. All knowledge is one. The best music is mathematics. The highest forms of design are in science. It is
impossible to study literature without a knowledge of the
history of the period involved. History is meaningless without
a knowledge of economics. All these are bound together by
the media of speech and logic. Where in the circuit of
oneness do you start?

The answer we have recommended is to "throw away your
watch and do as you please." The next few pages offer a
"game of solitaire" to be played with honesty. This is called
an "Interest Indicator." It will not define the specific subject
area in which you should major and later seek a job. If, for
example, you think you want to teach, the "Interest Indicator"
will not prove that that is a right or a wrong road to take.
All it can do is to challenge you to think about the many subjects to be explored in relation to your particular personality
and abilities.

The "Interest Indicator" has no scientifically established
reliability, no statistical validity. We can only point to the
fact that it has been useful in helping students to recognize
their intellectual interests, so far as they knew them at the
time. The "Interest Indicator" substitutes for a prolonged conversation with a college adviser, or can prepare you for a
conference. Perhaps your major choice determines the school
in your university from which you will receive a degree. The
following pages offer the opportunity to run furrows through
your thinking, to plough into your subconscious and come up
with a decision which will be right for you. Use a pencil, you
may wish to go through the forms a second time.

---

[2]Hutchins, Robert M., *Education for Freedom*. Louisiana State University
Press, Baton Rouge, Louisiana, 1943, p. 55.

INTEREST INDICATOR[3]

The college curriculum has been arbitrarily divided into three areas. Under each of the three sections of the "Interest Indicator" are ten questions which explore that subject area. Mark questions interesting you the most 1; those of second-rate interest mark 2; third in degree of interest mark 3 and for those in which you are definitely not interested mark 0. Transfer scores from each section to the final score sheet on page 15 and follow directions.

Section I—Sciences

—— 1. Would you like to learn about the characteristics of solids, liquids and gases, their relationships to one another, and laws governing their transformations?

—— 2. Would you like to study physical problems involving mathematical formulae?

—— 3. Do you want to know about the origin or formation of such scenic features as the Grand Canyon, Mammoth Cave, the Dells, the Garden of the Gods? Would you like to know about ocean currents, how a storm begins, where it goes and how it ends?

—— 4. Would you like to discover how synthetic materials are made?

—— 5. Would you enjoy systematizing scientific knowledge for the use of others?

—— 6. Do you have patience to repeat a laboratory experiment until it is exactly right?

—— 7. Would you like to study plant and animal life and their interrelationships? Would you like to study the physical aspects of the animal kingdom?

—— 8. Would you like to investigate the development and function of bodily processes and the relationship of these to body structure?

[3]The author wishes to acknowledge the contribution of questions by Edward H. Wells, chief actuary of Mutual Life Insurance Company; Helen M. Miller, employment counselor for the New York Chapter of the Registry of Medical Technologists and owner of the Miller Laboratory; and the faculty of Hunter College of the City of New York.

—— 9. Would you like to examine the minute structure of plant and animal cells?

——10. Would you like to learn about nutrition, growth, sanitation, health and disease?

Record here the total number of: First choices ——————
Second choices ——————
Third choices ——————
Zeros ——————

Section II—Social Sciences

—— 1. Would you like to find out why human beings behave as they do?

—— 2. Would you like to study large corporations, their history and how they function?

—— 3. Would you like to study the causes and cures of poverty?

—— 4. Would you like to understand how goods and services are produced and distributed?

—— 5. Would you like to study our country's heritage?

—— 6. Would you like to learn how peoples govern themselves?

—— 7. Would you like to study the development of human society and man's organized efforts to build a better society?

—— 8. Would you like to study primitive cultures?

—— 9. Would you like to study the problems of democracy?

——10. Would you like to understand the emotional problems of people?

Record here the total number of: First choices ——————
Second choices ——————
Third choices ——————
Zeros ——————

Section III—Humanities

—— 1. Would you like to read the best of man's recorded thoughts as found in great books?

—— 2. Would you like to learn how to evaluate the classics and modern literature?

—— 3. Would you like to study the language of music and how to write it?

—— 4. Would you like to study the natural bases of good design?

—— 5. Would you like to study the great social and political forces, and the relation of propaganda to them?

—— 6. Would you like to study the philosophies of the ancients?

—— 7. Would you like to learn other languages?

—— 8. Would you like to study the history and development of art?

—— 9. Would you like to study the relation of music to art?

——10. Would you like to study other peoples as revealed through their literature?

Record here the total number of: First choices ——

Second choices ——

Third choices ——

Zeros ——

How to Determine Score

SAMPLE FROM SECTION I—SOCIAL SCIENCES

Suppose you had {

1 No. Ones $\times$ 10 = 10
4 No. Twos $\times$ 5 = 20
4 No. Threes $\times$ 1 = 4
                  TOTAL = 34

1 No. Zeros to be subtracted from above total = 1

This will always be 10

Your Score for Section I = 33

After scoring yourself on the preceding three pages, fill in form on the next page.

Score Sheet

SECTION I

—— No. Ones $\times$ 10 = ———

—— No. Twos $\times$ 5 = ———

—— No. Threes $\times$ 1 = ———

                       TOTAL = ———

—— No. Zeros to be subtracted   = ———

        Score for Section I = ———

SECTION II

—— No. Ones $\times$ 10 = ———

—— No. Twos $\times$ 5 = ———

—— No. Threes $\times$ 1 = ———

                       TOTAL = ———

—— No. Zeros to be subtracted   = ———

        Score for Section II = ———

SECTION III

—— No. Ones $\times$ 10 = ———

—— No. Twos $\times$ 5 = ———

—— No. Threes $\times$ 1 = ———

                       TOTAL = ———

—— No. Zeros to be subtracted   = ———

        Score for Section III = ———

interpretation of interest indicator

Employers want trained minds and also maturing personalities. Following intellectual interests—wherever they may lead— is the best way to develop this vague thing called personality, the basic vocational tool. Proof of that is observation. There are so few areas in life where one may throw away his watch and do as he pleases that any opportunity to have a good time in the liberal arts curriculum should be utilized. The next time someone asks you, "Why in the world are you majoring in Latin?" answer them, "Because I want to!"

"What good is Latin these days?" the antagonist may continue, and you reply, "As good as anything—for me!"

The academic adventure recommended above compels you to keep vocationally alert and emotionally steady. If such freedom sends you on wild chases, first in one corner of the curriculum, then in another, with no plan, nothing accomplished, your elders who are shaking their heads will say, "I told you so. She should have taken nothing but practical courses; someone should have forced her to." They blame the educational system, but you know where the trouble really lies— you again. "Keeping vocationally alert" while catching up on the world's knowledge (by passing college examinations, for instance), need not take years of any young life. By knowing what to do to discover the essential things about yourself, and having a place to record these discoveries, you can keep vocationally alert as easily as you spend an allowance.

3

MOSTLY ABOUT COURSES

> *New professions for young people, new hope*
> *for the afflicted, new understanding of how*
> *science can serve for peace—these are among*
> *the items on the agenda of the present and im-*
> *mediate future.... But these things—and many*
> *others I might mention—are but a beginning.*
> *The door of knowledge is barely opened.*[1]
>
> —DAVID LILIENTHAL

THE FIRST STEP IN LEARNING ANYTHING new is to learn the names of objects. The baby learns the names of people: Mommy, Daddy. The school child learns the names of symbols: A, B, C. The college student does this for as many areas of specialization as are represented by the list of college courses. He learns the names, the nature and functions of symbols. So we, too, starting to learn about the vocational world will begin by learning the names of various duties or skills.

Medieval colleges divided their curriculum into the *trivium* and *quadrivium,* the *quadrivium* including mathematics. Today college courses are usually classified according to three, sometimes four categories.

I. SCIENCES

BOTANY	ZOOLOGY
PHYSIOLOGY	PHYSICS
ASTRONOMY	GEOLOGY
GEOGRAPHY	CHEMISTRY

MATHEMATICS

---

[1] Lilienthal, David, "Atomic Energy Is *Your* Business." *The New York Times Magazine,* January 11, 1948, p. 5.

17

II. SOCIAL SCIENCES	III. HUMANITIES
ECONOMICS	LANGUAGES
HISTORY	PHILOSOPHY
SOCIOLOGY	CLASSICS
POLITICAL SCIENCE	MUSIC
PSYCHOLOGY	FINE ARTS

Your particular college may not subscribe to this classification, but in general, these three categories comprise the liberal arts curriculum. At first thought, the relation of college courses to vocational names seems too vast to be considered. Who can foretell the vocational usefulness of any college study? President Shuster of Hunter College once said to a group of vocational counselors: "I cannot possibly imagine how I could have earned a living without the study of Greek, yet I cannot promise students a living just because they study it."

The categories given—Science, Social Sciences, Humanities—are offered to refine our problem, not to limit it, in order that we may start with one unit and lead out into the unfathomable riches of the liberal arts curriculum. In the spirit of research, then, we begin by learning occupation names. The next section of this chapter lists occupation titles which experience has shown have a relation to the courses named. Presented in this way, however, the list is misleading in one respect; it seems to indicate that each course is only "good for" the occupations designated under it. That is obviously not true, because every subject is "good for" a variety of vocations, depending upon you as well as on the analytical thought and hard work you give to its vocational application.[2]

It is obvious that as a student in any of the departments you might find a real vocational interest in some of the occupational titles listed under other categories. The point made clear in Chapter IV, where employers' specifications are given for some of these vocations, is that these categories are not mutually

---

[2]A test to use along with your search is the "Grace Manson Occupational Blank for Women," published by the Michigan School of Business, Ann Arbor, Michigan.

exclusive. So! If you want to major in zoology "just for the fun of it," as is said when an impressive reason can't be found for doing something one wants to do, by all means major in zoology and look for occupations more appealing elsewhere.

Suppose you are on a trip with the glee club and are entertained at a fraternity house, in a neighboring college. Your dinner partner remarks that he spent the past summer as a microscopist for an oil company. He's food for this vocational guidance book you are writing! Do you know who a microscopist is and what he does? This book is not hidden away in your evening bag, but remember "microscopist" when you get back to college—and this diary. What a microscopist does can be dug up elsewhere, unless, of course, the dinner partner is eager to explain on the spot. He probably is. Well, anyway, you could ask him. You will probably decide that starting out as a microscopist for an oil company is not for you. But how about some of those other titles, discovered in other places?

If you work at this game at all, you will unearth many such names. Somewhere along the line you will find a title which makes you want to know a great deal more about the job it labels. Trust your feelings and judgment. You will make mistakes, and start up avenues of search which become dead ends for you particularly—not necessarily so for another person. But isn't it better to learn in this fashion than to be a vocational blank at graduation? Only by practice can you learn how to trust feelings. If you are interested, or think you are interested, investigate! What vocational research can be accomplished at one football dance, at one YWCA meeting, at one anything! Actually, the job titles which might be associated with any course are too numerous to mention. The mere attempt to list a few is like trying to describe the universe with examples. Your own discoveries will mean more to you than those listed here, for the valid reason that they are personal discoveries, not something done for you.

As a rule, the liberal arts student has left her (and his) vocational thinking to be done in the employer's applicant chair—on the spot. No wonder the employer, having no vivid recollection of his own vocational youth, often considers the liberal arts curriculum "impractical" and thinks it "should be modernized."

SCIENCES

(List additional titles you discover in the blank space left in each division.)

Botany

Agricultural Economist
Agronomist
Biometrician
Nature Study Counselor
Plant Breeder
Plant Pathologist
Research Worker
Microscopist

Zoology

Animal Breeder
Apiculturist
Biologist
Entomologist
Technician

Physiology and Biology

Biologist
Medical Pathologist
Nurse
Physician
Anthropologist

Physics and Astronomy

Technician
Engineer
Airplane Designer
Air Travel (pilot, navigator,
    weather forecaster)

Geography and Geology

Technician
Soil Analyst
Cartographer
Survey Soil Worker

Mathematics

Technician
Teacher
Industrial Researcher

Chemistry

Technician in:
  Foods
  Clothing
  Oils
  Synthetics
  Medicine
  Textile Manufacture

SOCIAL SCIENCES

*(List additional titles you discover in the blank space left
in each division.)*

Economics and History

Accountant Analyst
Census Taker
Buyer
Merchandising Counselor
Business Forecaster
Economist
Researcher

Political Science and Sociology

Consular Agent
Journalist
Industrial Hygienist
Social Service Worker
Anthropologist

Psychology

Counselor
Nursery School Teacher
Psychiatrist
Psychologist
Personnel Worker

HUMANITIES

(List additional titles you discover in the blank space left in each division.)

Languages (including English)

Bibliographer
Interpreter
Editorial Worker
Reporter
Newspaper Feature Writer

Philosophy

Religious Educator
Social Service Worker

Art

Fashion Designer
Advertising Artist
Window Display Designer
Draftsman
Magazine and Book Illustrator

Classics

Bibliographer
Librarian
Teacher
Writer

Music

Singer
Musician
Teacher
Composer

PHYSICAL EDUCATION

Public Recreation Worker
Social Worker
Teacher

Your title discoveries may not be known now, but it is safe to say you will find a natural niche for any new occupations in one of the above divisions. If the material in these pages has made you conscious of the names given to occupations and stimulates you to find other titles, you are well on the way to a pay roll designation all your own. But this is just the beginning.

Does all this mean that you may go to an airplane factory and say, "I majored in philosophy, the classics, etc., and feel qualified for a job with your company"? Chapter IV says, "A thousand times no!" Chapter IV gives employers' specifications, in the employers' language so that you can learn to speak in terms of job skills, not college courses.

Actually, your first position will not be chosen entirely according to vocational interests, even if such interests could be definitely isolated and were real enough to photograph. Of course, if your talents are very obvious, then you are the one-in-ten girl whose choice will be inevitable. However, nine out of ten girls will ask these questions about any position: "Where is it located?" "Will I like the working conditions?" "What does my family think of it?" "How often can I get home?" Such questions will call for a compromise. But your need for a job is nonetheless urgent. Chapter IV shows how the employment market may be explored by the college woman. Read all the specifications and see if there are not at least a dozen places where your interests will fit—on the employer's terms, not on a schoolgirl's dreams.

4

TOOLS OF BUSINESS

IN YOUR STUDENT DAYS, your vocabulary is, naturally, concerned with courses. You say, "I have to study for an 'eko' exam" when talking about economics. Other daily chatter covers such abbreviations as "psych," "poly sci," and so forth. Subject majors, graduation requirements, grade points, honor credits, are ever-present topics of conversation, not to mention the extracurricular activities: Who is to be elected for student senate; who is in the cast of the new speech school play; who is your date for the senior prom?

The college campus jargon is being used rightfully for the expression of thoughts about yourself and about your coming place in the "outside employed world." But the employer in this "outside" world has a negative reaction to the applicant who comes to him, describing her real or imagined employment qualifications in terms of college life. The employer wants you to know *his* vocabulary, his specific requirements. How you should have become so informed, he could not tell you. Yet he does, indeed, expect you to use his language rather than one composed of courses, majors and extracurricular achievements. "I want to do personnel work because I have had a psychology course!" If the employer has heard that statement several times in one morning, he is likely to growl that he doesn't care what your major was or whether you ever went to college. "We want the 'personnel type of candidate' who knows our company."

Our hypothetical employer is like the jury in the Gilbert and Sullivan opera, *Trial by Jury.* You recall the twelve jurors listening to beautiful Edwin, the defendant, who is being sued by Angelina for breach of promise. Edwin admits that indeed he had loved "this young lady today and loved that young lady tomorrow." The jurors all nod and sing:

> *Oh I was like that as a lad!*
> *A shouting young thing of a rover;*

I behaved like a regular cad;
But that sort of thing is all over.
I am now a respectable chap
And shine with a virtue resplendent,
And therefore I haven't a rap
Of sympathy with the defendant!
Trial-la-law! Trial-la-law!
Singing so merrily Trial-la-law!

In all probability the employer who growls at you for using course names as though they were vocational tools, did the same thing when he was a lad, and has forgotten all about that in his "virtue resplendent," but said employer has a definite purpose, even if he seems unreasonable. He is saying that he doesn't care what courses you took, he is interested in the person. What can you contribute that his business requires?

These requirements, especially as they pertain to college women, are presented here in two categories: the "Tools of Business" and "Tools of the Professions." The basic business tools are, of course, typing, shorthand, bookkeeping, selling and clerical work. A single entrepreneur, doing all his own work, is the only business organization you will find without one or more of these skills being used by supplementary personnel.

As you will see from the following material, these skills are also extremely important because they can be used in numerous ways. Many of them are entree into a profession. Department store selling, for example, can open the door to the professional field of apparel merchandising; or being a secretary to an editor will give you background knowledge of the mechanics and vocabulary of publishing, should you decide on journalism. And, just as important, business tools may become a profession in themselves. That free-lance transcription office discussed on page 30 could become a thriving, permanent business; or, your interest in bookkeeping might lead you into the traffic field with its increasing professional opportunities.

"Must I be a typist, a stenographer, a bookkeeper?" you moan. "I thought this book was saying that the liberal arts curriculum was all the vocational tool I needed!" This workbook is, indeed, devoted to the proposition that the liberal arts studies furnish real techniques for life and living. There is, however, no substitute for constantly acquiring specific skills, and since the business and professional tools are so closely interrelated, at least read through these pages which are an introduction to the chapter concerning "Tools of the Professions." Then decide where and how you want to start out on your vocational trip.

TYPING POSITIONS FOR THE COLLEGE GIRL

If you did not learn to type in the fourth grade (which is really the proper age level when there is also the time to learn such a basic skill), you certainly have wished you were an accomplished typist by now. If you must be on someone's pay roll immediately after graduation (that is, within a matter of hours or days after receiving a diploma), the quickest route is often to offer typing skill in exchange for a salary check. A typist's ability can be tested immediately, can produce immediate results. You will not want to take just any available typing position, should you decide to use this skill. Some organizations say frankly that they do not wish to employ a college girl as a typist. She becomes restless too soon, thinks more about the promotion ahead than of the duty at hand, and, in addition, their experience has been that a college girl does not get along well with those of her colleagues who are high school graduates. These are real complaints. There are times, however, when the situation is reversed, as you shall see.

How good are you? You have been typing class assignments, but what is your performance, judged by commercial standards? Can you type for five minutes without making a single error? Test yourself once a week, for at least six weeks prior to that first employment-seeking venture. Note below your scores. (Speed is the total number of words written, minus ten words for every error made, divided by the number of minutes of the test.) Get a perfect score on this one.

FIRST TEST   SECOND TEST

Speed —————   Speed —————

Errors —————   Errors —————

THIRD TEST   FOURTH TEST

Speed ————   Speed ————

Errors ————   Errors ————

FIFTH TEST   SIXTH TEST

Speed ————   Speed ————

Errors ————   Errors ————

Don't be easy on yourself; you'll regret every excuse you make. If it seems impossible to be strictly accurate in judging your typing performance, put it down in your mental notebook that one of the greatest lessons life will teach you is entitled, "IIow to See Myself as Others See Me."

Typing Positions That Offer Experience

Title of Position: Correspondent.

Type of Organization Employing Correspondents: Many large department stores employ correspondents to answer customer mail. Book-of-the-Month Club employs recent college graduates to answer mail by dictating replies (which someone else types)[1] into a machine.

Kind of Experience Received in Exchange for Typing: Copywriter's approach to mail-order customers. Experienced copywriters may write the copy, but you are being trained in that skill all the while.

There is a good-sized department store near your home, college or in some nearby town. Your first assignment, as a cub reporter for this vocational information textbook, is to find out from at least one such department store:

1. Does the store employ correspondents?

---

[1] The personnel manager of the Book-of-the-Month Club said, "While we do not require our correspondents to be able to type, we do find that such ability facilitates employment. For example, if there is no correspondent position open when the girl applies, we can use her typing ability in a temporary position until such an opening occurs."

2. What additional duties, if any, does the correspondent have?

3. What previous experience is required for this position?

4. What are your own impressions about the organization, the people met, conditions observed?

5. What do you want to do about it?
   a. Brush up on your typing skill?
   b. Get a part-time position as a sales girl in a store?
   c. Spend a summer's vacation working in any capacity in such a store?

Title of Position: Manuscript Typist.

Kind of Experience Received: Direct contact with writing, authors and publishers. Typing edited manuscripts will familiarize you with many phases of editorial work as well as give you insight into the requirements determining the acceptance of a manuscript by a publisher.

Many state universities and some colleges have publishing houses where you could work while in school. Also, there are always professors writing books and graduate students needing their theses typed. The two largest publishing centers are, of course, New York and Chicago, but some trade journals and small book publishers are located throughout the country. These might provide summer work. Literary agents are mostly concentrated in New York and shouldn't be overlooked for that beginning typing job, should you come to the Gotham metropolis with publishing work your goal.

1. Does your college publish books? What are its requirements for a manuscript typist?

2. Is there a service on campus, specializing in the typing of research papers and theses? If not, why not start your own?

3. What publishing houses are located near enough to you to provide a job?

Title of Position: Free-Lance Transcriber.

Kind of Experience Received: Selling your own product; publicizing your own services; managing your own business.

You want to be your own boss? Have all the headaches, and all the profits? Clergymen, physicians, psychiatrists and other business and professional people are using with increasing frequency the Dictaphone, Ediphone, Sound Scriber and Audograph. Why not be the transcription service for them? Sound Scriber and Audograph plates may be mailed easily, and in this fashion your area of service is greatly enlarged. The usual college girl's independent venture is the tearoom, the rental library. A specialized transcribing service is as necessary—and different. Write to the offices of the machines mentioned above; they have branch offices which can help you form a nucleus of clients and provide information about the cost of equipment.[2]

To spark your imagination, this section about positions for the college girl, where typing is a "must," includes specifications from two employers. First we quote from *Opportunities for You in Air Transportation,* a booklet prepared by the American Airlines,[3] which will be sent upon request; perhaps the college library already has a copy. "Probably the most important qualification for a typist (beyond a high degree of accuracy and a fair degree of speed) is that she know how to set up statistical matter in tabular form. She will also be required to type manuscripts and form letters." The New York Stock Exchange requires that a "receptionist . . . be a good typist; 60 words a minute."

In the preceding pages we assumed you had decided, for reasons sufficient unto yourself, to use typing ability as a business tool. Now we may conclude the discussion of this first, and perhaps simplest, skill by asking you to consider:

---

[2]Dictaphone Corporation, 420 Lexington Avenue, New York, N. Y.; Ediphone Corporation, 10 East 40th Street, New York, N. Y.; Sound Scriber Corporation, 292 Madison Avenue, New York, N. Y.; Audograph Company of New York, 230 Park Avenue, New York, N. Y.

[3]American Airlines, 132 East 42nd Street, New York, N. Y.

1. In how many of these jobs have you had experience: addressing envelopes, filling in form letters, typing legal documents, statistics, manuscripts, order forms and catalogue cards?

2. What are the immediate vocational advantages in being a skilled typist?

3. How do you plan to use typing skill in the future?

STENOGRAPHIC POSITIONS
FOR THE COLLEGE GIRL

Stenography is, indeed, *The Road to Anywhere*,[4] as Frances Maule explains in her excellent little book which tells of the exalted positions some girls have achieved by beginning their

---

[4]Maule, Frances, *The Road to Anywhere*. Funk and Wagnalls, New York, 1938.

careers with stenography. The personnel manager of *Mademoiselle* also adds: "Don't forget that as a secretary you work for people who know and from whom you can learn. Other jobs open to beginners are usually clerical where the chance to learn by working with those who know is a great deal more remote."

Any high school girl can learn stenography, but seldom is she mature enough to be a good secretary at graduation time. You, a college girl, are, because of added maturity, judgment and competency. After having lived with this workbook and with yourself through college, you will certainly have some idea as to whether you want to use stenography merely as a beginning step to an executive's position, or to have a promotion come through increasingly responsible secretarial assignments. If it is to be the former, choose for early employers concerns where the secretary occasionally does take over the executive's work (*Mademoiselle,* for instance—next chapter). If you plan the other course, that is, being a secretary to a minor official at first and then to an executive with greater responsibility, the largest organization you can find near home is probably better. It will offer steady advancement in the secretarial field.

The personnel director of The Associated Press expresses the opinion of highly specialized companies when he states:

Our qualifications for a stenographer are concerned with her competency to take dictation and transcribe it efficiently. We prefer she have a liberal arts degree, but that combination is hard to find. We do prize the qualifications represented by a college degree, a college-type personality assumed, plus stenographic competency. At least she must be a high school graduate from an academic course. Promotion is to more responsible secretarial desks. A stenographer seldom becomes a reporter.

Although a stenographer rarely jumps the barriers in large organizations, there are more small companies than large in this world. Look around to see what the promotional opportunities are in any particular company. List the names of two companies, like The Associated Press, which say promotion for secretaries is usually to more responsible secretarial duties, seldom over to the dictating part of the job.

Companies offering "Associated Press type" of promotion:	Companies offering "road to anywhere type" of promotion:
1.	1. ....
2.	2. ....

Some free day, investigate to see if the guesses made above are really true.

In contrast to the restrictions of The Associated Press, "once-in-the-stenographic-department-seldom-anywhere-else," the National Broadcasting Company, Inc., encourages promotion in line with special aptitudes. NBC says: "Employees who started as stenographers and secretaries now include: administrative assistant, employment manager, executive officer's secretary, junior press writer, office manager, play reader, sales service manager, script editor. As a matter of fact NBC's promotion-from-within policy functions so well that most of our major executive positions are filled by employees who grew up within the company."[5]

There is a radio station near you. Visit the studios and find out:

1. What duties in addition to stenographic, does the secretary perform?

2. What new skills is she learning on the job?

3. Of what chain is this station a member?

[5]*National Broadcasting Company Job Inventory,* booklet sent free on request. National Broadcasting Company, 30 Rockefeller Plaza, Room 505, New York, N. Y.

Some Basic Stenographic Qualifications

Rockefeller Institute for Medical Research: Secretary. Needs ability to take shorthand and to type, and a technical vocabulary, either in the fields of biology, chemistry or medicine. A knowledge of French and German is desirable. Personal qualifications are important.

New York Stock Exchange: Secretary. Some experience as a secretary in the financial field plus ability to pass a dictation test at a minimum of 120 words per minute. The majority choose to remain with the Exchange, but these girls do have opportunities to make contacts for promotional openings in firms which are members of the Exchange. We require the wholesome college type who has a quiet confidence in her own ability, is friendly, cooperative, resourceful.

American Airlines: Airlines select general office workers carefully. As a general rule, airlines promote from their own ranks. A secretary is usually selected from the general stenographic group. She must be able to type at least 60 words a minute and take dictation at 110 to 120 words per minute. She will probably be given specialized training to meet the needs of her department. If she is a secretary in an airline accounting department, for example, she will have some knowledge of accounting. Her judgment must be good, her knowledge of the English language broad. She must be accurate and trustworthy, because often she will have to sign her employer's letters and make decisions in his absence. She should have some knowledge of filing and record-keeping. Because a secretary often has to meet her employer's visitors, she must be neat and well-poised and have a pleasing personality.

Institute for Juvenile Research, Chicago: Secretary. We are interested if the secretary, besides being an efficient stenographer, has done her college work in psychology or some related field. Her only promotion with us is as a secretary.

Of particular interest to the college girl who is thinking about stenography as a beginning tool, is the machine technique of taking dictation. The machine, stenotype, for example, attains greater speeds with less physical strain than is possible with manual stenography. A speed of 150 words is average on the stenotype machine. Average for manual is 100 words per minute. There are advantages in each. Find out what they are—for you. Bilingual ability on the stenotype machine opens the way to many careers in the secretarial field at home and abroad. Write to the Stenotype Company, 292 Madison Avenue, New York, N. Y., for information about this kind of shorthand and their office in your locality. They will tell you about Miss Sibyl Sills, founder of the Sills Reporting Service, who takes dictation in five languages. The manual stenographic companies, Gregg and Pitman, also have many branch offices. Compare their offerings with what the Stenotype Company has to say.

CLERICAL POSITIONS
FOR THE COLLEGE GIRL

Clerical work depends very much upon the health of the economic market. The college girl asking for clerical duties usually has in mind tasks which do not involve typing or stenography. In times of prosperity employers do have such positions. When economizing they are likely to require a clerk to be a stenographer, bookkeeper, to translate catalogues into French and German, to replace the receptionist who operates the office switchboard. There is no end to the requirements for the clerical position, when the employer is economizing. Then, too, except for such positions as are described below, the employer expects the college girl to be something more than a clerk. "You ought to know better," he seems to say to the college girl. "If you choose to marshal your abilities for a clerical position, that is your privilege, risk and business."

One Company and Its Clerical Jobs[6]

Music Cataloguer: Types catalogue cards; makes cross-reference cards for exclusive artists' orchestrations, standard orchestrations, collections of instrumental and vocal numbers, popular music, original music written by composers; files catalogue cards in music files. Prerequisites, typing, plus knowledge of popular and classical music.

Program Contact Clerk: Checks with conductors, artists, production directors to obtain and record titles, etc. in weekly log of all musical compositions to be broadcast. Prerequisite, music background. Minimum experience, one year of business experience, preferably in the music field.

Booking and Auditions Clerk: Schedules appointments for auditions and interviews persons who wish to discuss auditions; attends committee auditions; books casts for programs; informs cast of time and place of rehearsal and notifies talent of cancellation of program or rehearsal. Minimum experience, at least three years' production experience desirable and additional theatrical experience helpful.

Record Clerk: Performs clerical and typing duties in connection with the maintenance of personnel records. Prerequisites, high school diploma, typing. Minimum experience, no experience necessary but one year preferred.

Budget Clerk: Maintains record of proposed and actual operating expenses; maintains receipt records; carries on correspondence regarding accounts. Prerequisite, high school diploma but college degree preferred. Minimum experience, one year in budget or related field.

Publicity File Clerk: Maintains publicity information files showing names of all advertising agencies, clients, trade papers, radio stations desiring NBC publicity. Prerequisites, high school diploma and typing. Minimum experience, one to two years of general office work.

---

[6]Job descriptions from *National Broadcasting Company Job Inventory.* Booklet sent free on request. National Broadcasting Company, Inc., 30 Rockefeller Plaza, Room 505, New York, N. Y.

If you want employment as a clerk ask yourself such questions as:

1. What specialty have I? Music? Travel? Publicity?

2. What organizations deal with these specialties? (Begin in your own backyard and work out to the coast, east or west.)

3. What reasons do I have for choosing clerical work? (If you record them you may be able to see how realistic such reasons are.) Whatever they are, put them down.

4. Conclusions.

BOOKKEEPING POSITIONS
FOR THE COLLEGE GIRL

Bookkeeping, obviously, is essential in every business enterprise, and in professional practice. You may also want to consider the related fields of accountancy, statistics, etc.

Sampling the Variety of Bookkeeping Jobs

Burroughs Adding Machine Company: College women are trained to teach the operation of these machines to business houses which have purchased equipment. Called "field instructors," they sell the use of the machines by teaching how they operate. Burroughs considers this a very important position. Emphasis is placed upon pleasant personality, mature judgment and creative ability along business lines.

New York Stock Exchange: Bookkeeper. Special training and enthusiasm for detail, and advanced bookkeeping knowledge. Accountant. General accounting training, plus special study usually taken on the job.

Investment Houses and Some Banks: College women are trained, by some of these institutions, to work in their trust division. A college girl who meets their personality requirements and has a solid foundation in bookkeeping and in economics, and is interested, may be sent at the firm's expense, to study fiduciary accounting at a nearby university's evening session. The career of a trust officer is one which banking houses are opening to women for the simple reason that the women are the ones who have money left to them in trust. This is "working your way up" in the trust officer's profession. Entrance is also made possible by a law degree with specialization in trusteeships. The small town home bank or the not-so-small local bank can both offer excellent experience to the beginner. You are impressed by the experience offered by large institutions? They will be impressed by recommendations coming from the smaller bank, and you will know more about what you want and don't want, if early experience is obtained in a small organization.

The Traffic Field[7]: This field is both an internal and external operation which includes the traffic department of industrial firms, the job of which it is to arrange for transportation of the product, and the railroad, steamship, airline and truck transportation agencies that do the actual transporting.

Rate Clerk. This is a highly technical job which requires the background of a traffic course or a certificate from a traffic school. College girls, or beginning workers without college degrees, however, are sometimes trained as clerks. Essential is an ability to work with figures, liking for infinite detail, interest in the legal aspects of interstate and international trade. Promotion, made by passing "bar" examinations, is to the superior brackets of junior rate clerk, senior rate clerk, advanced rate clerk, assistant traffic manager, traffic manager.

General Positions. Here are found the ever-present stenographer, typist. Promotion is possible from these beginning positions, depending upon the personal qualifications and training of the worker, to the advanced category of sales, public relations, cost or sales analyst. The qualifications for this last position are exacting as far as personality requirements are concerned and so far as technical knowledge is involved.

Fill out the summary sheet on the next page if you want to start somewhere in the bookkeeping field.

---

[7]This service is not in itself new, but the professional standing of employees in it is now. Like clerks who formerly just read law until they knew enough to practice it, so traffic clerks have read, and in a great many places still do "read traffic law," until at long last promoted to traffic managership. Just as there are now law schools and bar examinations, so there are traffic schools and traffic examinations. These professional aspects are not yet universally accepted. Various groups are interested in training college girls for the traffic field on a professional basis.

1. What bookkeeping experience have you had? Describe in detail what you did, where; what accounts were kept, for whom. Was it paid work or voluntary duty, such as being treasurer for a Sunday school class?

2. Are any of the occupational titles which are given in Chapter III, or which you have discovered, concerned with bookkeeping in any way? If so, name them.

3. What about bookkeeping did you most enjoy? Keeping records, making the puzzle come out even, or the relationships it offered with the people concerned?

4. Do you think you are the expert bookkeeper, New York Stock Exchange type? Or do you think the public-relations-system teaching assignment of Burroughs would make you happier? What can you do about it?

SELLING POSITIONS
FOR THE COLLEGE GIRL

So near at hand is this world of selling that it is at times lightly considered. The sales position of "field instructor" at Burroughs has just been described. In the professional section other selling jobs are given under these titles: travel agent, fashion promotion, advertising writer, public relations. Either you are good and earn a high salary, or you are not so good, and eventually leave selling duties. If you are "sales minded," enjoying the vigor, push and competition, you'll succeed. You don't know? Why not find out?

1. What selling experience have you had? On the campus? For the yearbook? In a local store?

2. Did you enjoy it? Not what did your parents think, but did you really enjoy that relation with people? Record these feelings, pro and con.

The next chapter considers the vocational start through specializations other than those mentioned in "Tools of Business." Where do you belong? Why? Understand your reaction to these two ways of beginning a career. Above all, know that you have feelings in the matter.

5

TOOLS OF THE PROFESSIONS

WHEN YOUR VOCATIONAL ASPIRATIONS were in the vague stage mentioned in the first chapter (a vague stage which may endure some years after college), your thoughts were expressed like this: "I'd love something connected with radio"; or "I want something in my department [social sciences]." We have tried to give that "something" exact names in the preceding chapter about business tools. Now let's do the same thing for the professions.

New books are written every year describing specific occupations, but most important of all will be leads discovered when you ask, "I wonder what job titles that profession has for young college women?" When you do that kind of creative thinking and begin collecting that kind of personalized and definite information, you will be thrilled to see how everything from being a baby-sitter to taking a dog for a walk can add to vocational competency. You may find that special path where no one, especially a woman, has ever trod before.

For example, during the early 1930's, when all jobs were frozen, and general fear had completely paralyzed the employment market, women members of a local group characterized by their name, "Home Economics Women in Business," were besieged by requests from new home economics graduates to tell them how to get started in the field. At one meeting members were discussing the tragedies each saw enacted daily, and finally one member said, "Why don't we just tell these girls that there are no positions open until some of us die? Why do we go on encouraging them to enter our field when we know it is closed? We like our jobs, but we know there are none like them needing new workers."

It was a challenging speech which relieved the tense situation by presenting a solution to their combined harassment.

Well, why not discontinue home economics training? "Wait a minute," exclaimed a member as she stood up. "Didn't each one of you *make* your own job? Did that job exist before you visualized it and took the trouble to investigate how your individual skills might be commercially profitable to a manufacturer? These new girls can do the same. The commercial world is in a spasm now, but it won't always be." So with this faith they continued to assure students that there would be a need for skilled home economists. Their service to society in so doing can never be estimated, as the Red Cross, the Department of Agriculture and all the war agencies in the 1940's who used home economists will testify.

Obviously, business tools may be more easily acquired, more quickly learned than those of the professions, because the latter are usually thought to require graduate specialization. Many of them do. Think about all of Chapter IV, and decide whether it will be necessary for you to acquire a business tool in order to pay for graduate specialization. Perhaps you are among the fortunate few who can go directly into graduate preparation without the help of a business tool. Or, you may be in the group which chooses to make business its profession. You will need help—self-help, or maybe self-help in enlisting the aid of others. If you discover special interests within yourself, then you may find a group of professional women who are willing and eager to help you along the way.

professional interest groups

In whatever city you wish to be employed you will probably find such organizations as: American Association of Women Accountants; National Foundation for Infantile Paralysis; Advertising Women of New York City; Filing Supervisors Association; American Association of Clinical Pathologists; The Society of American Florists; National Federation of Business and Professional Women's Clubs; The Women's Advanced Traffic Agents Club; Special Libraries Association; American Association of University Women; the Altrusans.

These groups, and others like them, sponsor college girls in various ways, some by offering them employment in their special field and providing tuition for evening graduate study. Others provide outright scholarships for vocational courses. They are powerfully effective groups to have as friends. They will admire you if you begin early to make their acquaintance by letter; learn their purpose and function, and little by little become acquainted with the officers personally. Too much work? You won't be worth their help unless you take the initiative. You'll find these groups through your dean's office, the Chamber of Commerce or through publications.

trade magazines

As each occupation has its organization, so each club, trade or hobby generally has its own magazine. Consulting *N. W. Ayer & Son's Directory of Newspapers and Periodicals* for publications in the field which interests you, will enlarge your horizon immeasurably. There is no better way to learn the vocabulary of industries, business and professions.

graduate schools

Scholarships are available in most of the graduate schools throughout the country—and abroad. The first and most obvious thing to do after you have decided to take graduate work in a particular subject, is to write to that department in several schools to see what their requirements are for financial assistance.[1] Their catalogues list the federal aids to which they have access. Your major professors, also, know of these helps, and the dean's office has bulletins about them. Ask, or write directly, for the booklet, *Financial Aids for College Students,* U. S. Office of Education, Washington, D. C.

In the following sections job titles are given which will be useful in themselves. Some require that fifth year of graduate work for the start, others for promotion—but again the part you supply will be the most important.

---

[1]Lovejoy, Clarence E., *Lovejoy's Complete Guide to American Colleges and Universities.* Simon and Schuster, New York, 1948.

SOCIAL SCIENCES

Any line separating careers in the social sciences from those in the humanities must be purely imaginary. But like the equator, the division serves an organizational purpose. Because your college catalogue probably places certain majors in the social science division and others in the humanities, this workbook has the temerity to divide careers into similar groupings.

If you major in the social sciences, you do so because that discipline interests you more than the others, but you are not shutting yourself off from occupations in the humanities. You might even be interested in some of those found in the science division. Here we will discuss social science careers as though they differed greatly from others. Is the practice of psychiatry a scientific occupation or a social science vocation? It is both. So it is with the following jobs and with those which you dig up through your own perseverance.

Wherever possible, with each job title, we have included comments from an actual employer: his requirements for the job itself; his suggestions concerning courses and experience that would be helpful in fulfilling the requirements; and his evaluation of the personality needed. Naturally, no one employer is the "final authority," but you will find that these specifications can be used as a foundation for many related fields.

Teaching

The first great profession for the college girl is, of course, teaching. Your own school has more information about that than any one book can give. The department of education in your college will direct you to sources of information about teaching opportunities, such as: placement offices of teachers' colleges; the professional office of the state employment service; metropolitan teacher-placement agencies. The Office of Education, Washington, D. C., can give you a nationwide view of educational needs and, also, refer you to special teaching assignments in our own territories and abroad.

If you choose not to enter the profession as a teacher, you most certainly will take an active part as a citizen, working to improve the teaching situation in your community. We have enough knowledge to take the next step. We do not need to keep repeating our blunders, continue deadening the precious minds of the children entrusted to our schools. We do not need to have an alarming shortage of teachers. We know how to make teaching the thrilling profession it really should be for teacher and student. Somewhere in this never-ending struggle to apply what is known to improve the lives and minds of the teachers and the taught, somewhere as teacher or citizen, you will find your own place of service. Here, however, is one new and developing teaching area which can act as a stimulus to further thinking.

Job Title: Nursery School Teacher.

Employer: International Nursery School, United Nations, Lake Success, New York.

Courses Needed: A college degree plus any specialization which reflects an interest in children. A scientific specialization could be preparation for this field, depending upon the candidate's personality; also helpful are courses in art, clay modeling, painting, handcrafts, woodwork, music and music appreciation. Foreign languages are necessary for work in nursery schools in foreign-speaking communities. Courses in general psychology, child psychology and sociology reflect the inherent interest of the applicant.

Personality Requirements: A good nursery teacher has a background of culture so that she can inspire children to enriched living. Formal training is the framework upon which she has built her personality. Does she respect children as individuals? Applicants are also usually judged on (1) personal adjustment to life, balance and maturity; (2) creative activities beyond the pattern of daily routine; (3) specific training and experience with children.

Experience Helpful: Mother's helper, baby-sitter. Working with groups. Summer camp counselor work is helpful in defining the applicant's interests as well as the answers to "Why do you believe nursery school training is important?" "What books and magazines have you read in this field?"

Background Reading: Landreth, Catherine, *The Education of the Young Child.* John Wiley & Sons, New York, 1942.

Parents' Magazine, 52 Vanderbilt Ave., New York, N. Y.

Foster, Josephine C., and Mattson, Marion L., *Nursery School Education.* D. Appleton-Century, New York, 1939.

Alschuler, Rose, editor, *Children's Centers.* National Commission for Young Children. William Morrow and Company, New York, 1943.

YOUR DISCOVERIES NOTED HERE

In making discoveries, be careful to mark a difference between the nursery school which merely takes children off the mothers' hands for a certain number of hours a day—they are rightfully called "parking places for children"—and the type which offers outlets to the professionally trained college girl. This latter type is the school equipped with the proper indoor and outdoor play materials to encourage good physical development and in which the staff is interested in the behavior patterns of the children, watching the social and emotional growth of each one. It may be that you will have to start your own. The "parking" types are more frequently found. By no means should they be called "nursery schools."

1. Name of School Visited:

2. Name of Person Interviewed:

3. College Courses Recommended:

4. Personality Requirements:

5. Experience Helpful:

6. Background Reading:

Psychology

It has taken a second global war to make humanity realize the importance of all the truths discovered about human emotions and the subconscious mind. That we can start with the individual's problems, and from there improve relations between individual and individual, from individual out into city, state, nation and the world is a marvelous realization. In his 1945 William Alanson White Memorial Lecture, Dr. G. B. Chisholm said:

The responsibility for charting the necessary changes in human behaviour rests clearly on the sciences working in that field. Psychologists, psychiatrists, sociologists, economists and politicians must face this responsibility. It cannot be avoided. Even a decision not to interfere is still a decision and carries no less responsibility.[2]

---

[2]Chisholm, G.B., "The Re-establishment of Peacetime Society," *The Psychiatry of Enduring Peace and Social Progress.* The William Alanson White Memorial Lectures, 1711 Rhode Island Avenue, Washington, D. C., 40 cents each.

United Nations Educational, Scientific and Cultural Organization, 405 East 42nd Street, New York, N. Y., will send you details concerning world-wide plans for the field of child and adult education in mental hygiene.

We have the knowledge, it has always been available. Now we are beginning to use that knowledge. From an academic interest in the workings of the human mind and emotions, we have passed to a functional appreciation of psychology. Since World War II we are timidly daring to use that knowledge to cure ills of long ignorance. The curing stage is realistically called "dynamic psychology." If you are interested in the curative end of psychological truths, if you want to know how to help straighten twisted personalities, you will need first a medical degree, then psychiatric or psychoanalytic training, or a graduate degree in psychology or social case work.

Graduate specialization is your first concern if psychology interests you as a profession. While you are deciding among the possible choices of graduate work in educational psychology, social work and medicine, ask at a near-by hospital if they employ clerks in their psychiatric departments. These clerks are sometimes called aides. The salaries are always meager, but the experience is rewarding. The director of social work at your state capital can tell you which hospitals employ aides. Browse around to see what your city, county and state have to offer in advice, information and jobs. This could be a summer occupation if you can find a hospital that will take an undergraduate as aide.

Write to Child Study Association, 221 West 57th Street, New York, N. Y., for a list of camps where you might be employed as a counselor. The Camp Department of *Parents'* Magazine, 52 Vanderbilt Avenue, New York, N. Y., will also help. Write early in January, prior to the summer you plan to spend as a counselor. Such experience can serve as initial preparation for the career of child guidance counselor, for which you will ultimately need both a degree from a recognized school of social service and graduate work in psychiatric social service. Here are several employers' requirements to think about:

Institute for Juvenile Research, Division of the Department of Public Welfare, State of Illinois: Psychiatrist. M.D. from a recognized medical school; three years' experience

in psychiatry, one of which must have been in child
psychiatry.

Institute for Psychoanalysis, Chicago, Illinois: Psychologist.
M.A. degree in psychology, with experience in clinical
psychology.

YOUR DISCOVERIES NOTED HERE

(Also, keep a record of all the group activities in which you
took an active part. Grade yourself on how well, or poorly you
worked with others; did you insist upon dominating the group,
or did you really work with colleagues?)

Personnel

In placing emphasis on psychology courses as a vocational
tool, be sure you know the employer; sometimes he likes
them as such, and sometimes he doesn't. "It always annoys
me," said one personnel director, "to have the applicant consider a psychology major equipment for a personnel job. We

want applicants who know our company or are willing to begin in jobs where they will learn about the company." When you stop to think about it, you can readily understand that a psychology major can be preparation for any and every job in the world—like the whole liberal arts curriculum. You must give vocational thought to every major.

Job Title: Personnel Clerk.

Employer: Esso Standard Oil Company.

Courses Needed: College graduate preferable.

Other Qualifications: Shorthand, at least 100 words per minute; intelligent curiosity; ability to handle detail; enthusiasm.

Description of Work:

1. Interviews all applicants for routine positions.
2. Selects qualified candidates for jobs and arranges interviews with office manager.
3. Handles employment details for accepted applicants. This involves checking necessity for working papers, expediting completion of medical examinations, arranging date to begin work, etc.
4. Tests typists and comptometer operators.
5. Briefly outlines company policy to new employees.
6. Advises employees regarding requests for transfer or personal problems, referring special cases to personnel manager or personnel assistant.
7. Contacts outside sources, such as agencies, business schools, etc., regarding candidates for employment.
8. Answers correspondence concerning applicants.
9. Hires practically all service staff employees.
10. Maintains constant check with department where service staff employees are placed to keep informed of absences, changes in status, etc., in order to inform treasurer's department when necessary.
11. Trains junior clerk.

12. Checks all new files when made up to be sure that the necessary information has been obtained and expedites incomplete cases.

13. Reviews all completed references on new employees before sending to specific department for review.

14. Administers vacation program. This involves sending letters to all departments regarding the number of vacation substitutes required and arranging to cover vacation calls with qualified service staff employees.

15. Develops new systems and procedures for more efficient operation of the office.

Job Title: Personnel Interviewer.

Employer: Time, Inc.

Courses Needed: Any college course is as good as another, depending upon the student. She needs a broad cultural background.

Personality Requirements: A lively curiosity about everything one sees, hears, meets. Ability to keep reasonably alert about what is going on in the world, and what has been going on. *Breadth* of learning is of more use to the beginning worker than *depth* of learning. We are interested in the whole personality of the applicant. For example, we are interested in what the girl did in college and what she did with her vacations, more as an indication of the mental and vocational alertness of the applicant, than because what she may have done might parallel any of our duties here.

Experience Needed: Once we did give preference to applicants who had taken graduate training in the personnel field, but we found that a girl coming from within the organization (from a stenographic, typist or clerical position), does a better job. A personnel interviewer must be vocationally mature. She knows what routine work is, how one has to accept it; she knows there is no golden job, that an ideal job, if it does exist, has inherently boring aspects. She has had firsthand working experience in department store or office; she knows how other people live and have to work.

Job Title: Counselor.

Employers: Churches, High Schools, Colleges, YWCA, Social Service Institutions.

Courses Needed: A.B. or B.S. degree in any field of real interest to student. Master's degree in social case work.

Personality Requirements: Degrees are needed, and graduate specialization in guidance counseling is essential. All are of no avail unless such study has been built upon a personality which understands itself, a well-integrated emotional pattern; in other words, a person who enjoys working with people, who has respect for them as human beings.

Experience Needed: Leadership in any voluntary group associations, Sunday school, Girl Scouts, YWCA groups, college and high school extracurricular clubs—all these are excellent groundwork for graduate training.

Background Reading: Your best reading will be catalogues of universities offering graduate specialization in the counseling field. Be sure to inquire of your graduate school about fellowships offered in this department. Don't take it for granted that you just can't afford graduate specialization until you've tried every alternative.

Baxter, Edna, *An Approach to Guidance.* D. Appleton-Century, New York, 1946.

Job Title: Employment Counselor.

Employer: State Civil Service Commissions.

Courses Needed: Each state has its own requirements. College graduation is a usual prerequisite in New York State, but experience in the field is frequently allowed to substitute for a college degree.

Personality Requirements: You must enjoy working with people of all types, and have a thoroughgoing respect for all classes and personalities of mankind. Knowledge of labor problems, social problems of your own time and locality is essential. You must be able to endure routine and to work under pressure without passing on these frustrations to the client.

Experience Needed: Visit a state employment service[3] near your home and one near your college, if that is in a different locality, because the services of a local office are determined largely by the community served. Watch the interviewers at work and note the kinds of openings they are filling. You will then realize that it is essential to have knowledge of a large number of occupations. One way to learn about job requirements is to work in some of the occupations. Obviously you can't work at all of them, but actual participation in even a few jobs will be helpful. Selling in a department store and working as a camp counselor are two ways of gaining experience in dealing with people, a requisite of successful interviewing.

YOUR DISCOVERIES NOTED HERE

The job descriptions from Esso Standard Oil and Time, Inc., illustrate companies where graduate training or even a college degree are secondary to the business training of "a girl who has just plain worked." The job descriptions from the counselor's field and that of the employment interviewer place emphasis upon graduate training. Business experience helps, particularly in the employment interviewer's job, but graduate study in personnel fields receives major consideration.

1. Which appeals to you? The "business"   _____

                                The "professional"   _____

---

[3]Kaufmann, Fritz, *Your Job*, Chapter 13, "Directories of Federal and State Agencies." Harper, New York, 1948.

2. Why? Your reasons will change. They will grow in maturity as you grow. Keep a record of these whys.

3. Scout around to see what is offered in the personnel field, your favorite department store, for example, manufacturing plants, industrial firms and your own state employment service. Keep a record of those visits here.

Social Work

Does your biography record to date responsible activities in, say, the student YMCA-YWCA, the Community Chest or some other community organization? Leadership in this area doesn't make you a social worker, but if you enjoyed participating in such groups, it would be worth while to explore the field further to see if some vocational significance is present for you. Many forces are operating in modern society—economic, political, psychological—which disrupt normal living and bring about numerous problems to individuals, families and groups. Modern organized social work is directed toward helping people as individuals and as groups to attain satisfying relationships and standards of living in harmony with their own wishes and capacities as well as with the well-being of the community. It is also paramountly concerned with discovering and correcting the causes of these personal and community ills.

To give such help and services, many types and fields of social work, such as social case work (including family social work, child welfare, medical and psychiatric social work), group work and community organization are used. The American Association of Social Workers has a variety of information ready to send you about this "growing profession which needs thousands of new members."[4]

Job Titles: Family Social Worker, Child Welfare Worker, Psychiatric Social Worker, Medical Social Worker, Social Group Worker, Community Organization Worker, Social Research Worker, Social Administrator, Counselor. From the booklet, *Social Work as a Profession*[5], you will find other positions in which you can be employed after receiving special training.

Employers: Camp Fire Girls, Inc.; 4-H Clubs; Girl Scouts; Young Women's Christian Associations; National Federation of Settlements; Family Welfare Association; The Salvation Army; United Christian Youth Movement; American National Red Cross; Community Chest. These are only a few of the leading organizations requiring trained social workers. Other important employers are the city, county or state welfare departments, and recreation, social insurance, housing and religious education programs.

    [4]*Preprofessional Education for Social Work.* American Association of Schools of Social Work, 130 East 22nd Street, New York, N. Y.
    [5]*Social Work as a Profession.* American Association of Schools of Social Work, 1313 East 60th Street, Chicago, Illinois.

Courses Needed: College preparation may embrace any specialty; social work can use them all. If you never have been interested in working with people and choose to major in an exact science, for example, the admission's committee of a school of social work would question rather thoroughly your real interest in this vocation. The usual major is, of course, within the social sciences department, with emphasis on psychology, sociology, economics, etc. and, if possible, introductory social work courses. Naturally graduate professional education involving two years in an accredited school of social work is, in many cases, a necessary "finishing touch" because it provides the opportunity for field work practice under supervision. Work fellowships and scholarships are available[6] and they are usually given to those whose social work interests have been expressed in undergraduate years by work with people.

Personality Requirements: You will need to do considerable reading in this area, and again the American Association of Social Workers offers help through their various publications. Not only do you need to be interested in other people, but it is essential that you are able to communicate and demonstrate that interest to others—warmly and sincerely. A sense of humor plus judgment, mental and emotional balance, are also definite personality advantages.

Experience Needed: Experience, which could be obtained during the summer or as a part-time job or volunteer duty during the semester, could include: teaching crafts, etc., as a camp counselor; acting as a swimming or physical education instructor; working with your church's youth director on programming; assisting the program director of a public playground which has organized recreation; having dormitory responsibility on campus.

---

[6]*Social Work Fellowships and Scholarships.* American Association of Schools of Social Work, 130 East 22nd Street, New York, N. Y.

Description of Work:

"Family social work is one of the oldest and most basic types of service . . . which gives assistance in relation to situations where family friction, broken homes, economic distress, personality maladjustments, and similar difficulties are affecting individuals within a family group or the family as a whole. . . .

"Medical social workers collaborate with doctors and nurses in meeting social problems related to illness and medical care. . . .

"Social group work deals primarily with persons in their group relationships. Its greatest development has been in recreational and informal educational activities where the trained social worker functions chiefly as a supervisor of volunteer and paid leaders of groups. . . .

"Social research offers positions to those who have obtained education and experience in both social work practice and statistical and research methods . . . it is the primary function of research personnel to bring together facts for purposes of social planning."[7]

Background Reading:

The Social Worker. American Association of Schools of Social Work, 1313 East 60th Street, Chicago, Illinois.

Williamson, Margaret, *They Call Us a Group Work Agency.* The Woman's Press, New York, 1944.

Presenting Your Opportunity in a Youth Serving Organization. Youth Division, National Social Welfare Assembly, 134 East 56th Street, New York, N. Y.

Going Our Way? Leadership Services Department, National Board, YWCA, 600 Lexington Ave., New York, N. Y.

Trecker, Harleigh, *Social Group Work—Principles and Practices.* The Woman's Press, New York, 1948.

Coyle, Grace L., *Group Experience and Democratic Values.* The Woman's Press, New York, 1947.

---

[7]*Social Work as a Profession, op. cit.*

YOUR DISCOVERIES NOTED HERE

1. Do you make friends easily and feel at home with people of different races, color, ancestry, faiths, customs, social or economic background?

2. Do you have a keen interest in your community and its problems?

3. Do you like to go to meetings, work on committees, make public talks? (What experience have you had?)

4. What group work responsibility have you ever undertaken? Do you have ability to organize activities and take leadership among your schoolmates, in religious groups, in neighborhood and community programs?

Labor Relations

Everybody begins at a helpless stage and grows from infancy through the various stages of childhood and adolescence to maturity. Leaving the childhood stage is very painful for human beings. So it is with the institutions people manage. Collective bargaining between employers and employees is still in the infant stage. If you wish to help it continue to grow, to mature, there are three things you can do.

1. Become an expert in labor relations by taking graduate work in that field, either a Doctor's degree or at least some years of graduate study at universities offering such specialization. Become an expert in collective bargaining, labor law, labor history, wages, profits, prices, populations, national income, international trade and finance, and the economic and political organizations which deal with these subjects. (Note the courses now offered by Brookings Institute, Columbia University, New School for Social Research, University of Wisconsin and others.)

2. Join a union, if the job you are doing is represented by one. Become active in its affairs.

3. Seek employment with the Department of Labor, Washington, D. C. There may be a branch office near your home or college, because not all Department work is done in Washington. Write Washington for the job classifications they use. Of course, you know they employ stenographers, typists, clerks, etc., but there are other categories, such as statistician, public relations clerks, editorial workers. The Women's Bureau in the Department of Labor is another of the government bureaus which you should investigate. It works very closely with trade unions and, consequently, has information concerning job opportunities in that field for women. Another of your contacts should be the National Labor Relations Board, Washington, D. C.

YOUR DISCOVERIES NOTED HERE

Housing

Cities without slums! That particular cause of delinquency will vanish. Private capital and government money will place such slums in the same category as the stockade of witch-burning days. In the large housing units each particular duty will be performed by a specialist; in the smaller ones, beginners have greater opportunity. Your own investigation here will be most rewarding—a job for you, and interesting material for any sociology class. Find out what your city plans to offer in the two following categories:

Researchers: Economic and social fact-finders concerned with discovering what the community needs and what resources are available to supply these needs.

Management: All varieties of office help plus nursery school teachers, recreation group leaders and social workers.

There are two sources which you will need to study or consult for information, even if you have a housing project develop in your backyard. The library has a copy of the *National Association of Housing Officials Annual Report;* this is a directory of all official and unofficial housing agencies. The second resource is the Federal Civil Service at Washington, D. C.

Your Discoveries Noted Here

Ask Yourself:

1. "Why do I want a job in housing?" and write your answer.

2. What abilities do I have to offer?

Publishing

The road leading into publishing can be approached in
many ways, and once on that road, you will find that it has
many detours. Books, magazines, newspapers and trade journals comprise the main highway. Branching out from it, are
the allied fields of advertising, publicity, public relations and
art, so that the job possibilities are infinite. Writing and editing are the two activities which make all the others possible.
In this section, then, we shall travel only the main highway.

One basic comment needs to be made about writing in relation to the liberal arts curriculum. The majority of writing
courses in the English department emphasize the creative writing of fiction, poetry and essays. Through these courses you
can determine to some extent, at least, whether or not you
have writing talents. What you learn about writing simply
and directly, about composing any piece as a unit with a
beginning, middle and conclusion, will be your best carry-
over ability for the commercial field of publishing.

The majority of authors and editors are people who have
learned the techniques of a craft. The differences between this
craft and being able to write a term paper or a charming essay
are legion. The day-after-day work in journalism involves non-
fiction, feature articles, news stories, photograph captions,
advertising and other publicity copy, rewriting and editing
what other people write. Employees who are skilled in doing
these jobs well are the framework of publishing. To develop
such skills successfully, you must regard them as techniques
to be learned and not as inherent talents. The additional traits
which you will also need are: the ability to work well with
others no matter how great the deadline pressures are; the
ability to express yourself very clearly, vocally as well as in
writing; the capacity for being constantly aware of the world
around you and what is happening in it.

MAGAZINE PUBLISHING

Employer: Mademoiselle.[8]

General Requirements: Personality, good grooming and appearance are part of the battle for all jobs, and on a fashion magazine they assume even greater importance. This does not mean, however, that members of the staff must be walking fashion plates.

Because so much of the work of secretaries and assistants is telephone contact work with the public, advertisers and readers—and so much goodwill can be thereby generated —a good speaking voice and telephone personality are prerequisites and "blanket requirements." The ability to meet and work with people of varying temperaments helps greatly on a magazine where the various departments are so interdependent. In all departments there is an occasional necessity for overtime work during deadline periods, and all staff members must be able and willing to stay when they are needed.

General Qualifications of Assistants: Mademoiselle assistants frequently, although not always, start as secretaries, and so have secretarial skills. A college education or its equivalent is an essential. They must also be able to assume responsibility without close supervision, and, in writing jobs, have a willingness to do things over as many times as necessary. This must be done frequently in all magazine work.

Executive Assistant to Editor-in-Chief: Typing and shorthand. Initiative and ability to assume responsibility, to handle volume of detail and confidential material. Good knowledge of the workings of entire organization. General knowledge of publishing business and of fashion industry —manufacturers, stores, fabric houses, etc. Faculty for planning and organizing work. Good business sense. Di-

---

[8]The job specifications from *Mademoiselle* magazine are given in detail, because they illustrate so many of the basic elements involved in work for magazines, large or small.

plomacy, excellent memory for names and facts. Capacity for working long hours and under pressure.

Assistant to Managing Editor: Shorthand and typing. Initiative in handling correspondence, details, and in organizing work. A broad general background in arts, literature, current events, history, personalities. Writing ability. Editorial judgment. Ability to do competent research, accompany photographers, conduct intelligent interviews. General knowledge of whole magazine, work of all departments. General understanding of technical aspects of publication. Tact in relaying managing editor's requests to superiors.

Assistants to Associate Editor: Same as above, except for additional technical aspects. More emphasis on interviewing and supervising photography.

Assistant Fiction Editor: Typing and ability to handle correspondence. Good background in literature, both classical and modern; awareness of European influences and trends in writing; thorough knowledge of what other periodicals here and abroad are publishing. Good literary judgment, faculty for recognizing and encouraging new talent. Ability to deal with agents, publishers, writers. Speed at reading—and must enjoy it.

Assistant to Beauty Editor: Shorthand and typing. Ability to handle correspondence, keep records, follow through on details. Some writing talent. Interest in and general knowledge of cosmetics.

Assistants to the Jobs and Futures Editors: Same as assistants to the associate editor, with less emphasis on the literary and more on accurate, detailed research. First assistant need not have shorthand, but must have previous writing or editorial experience. Special talent for getting accurate, factual information.

Assistant to College Board Editor: Shorthand and typing. Ability to handle volume of correspondence, great deal of routine, detail work. Writing ability. Wide interest in education and the problems of college girls. Be able to mix well with college students and faculty.

Assistant to Design for Living Editor: Shorthand and typing. Capacity to assume a great deal of responsibility. Knowledge of home furnishings, merchandising.

Assistant to Travel Editor: Shorthand and typing. Ability to handle volume of correspondence. Interest in travel and in other countries. Knowledge of languages helpful.

Assistant to National Coordinating Director: Same as assistant to editor-in-chief, except that emphasis is on thorough knowledge of fashion connections rather than on publishing business. Merchandising and store selling experience necessary.

Assistant to Promotion Director: Typing. Writing experience and merchandising and fashion background, including retail store experience. Knowledge of fashion connections. Accuracy in handling detail work.

Assistant to Special Projects Editor: Shorthand and typing. Ability to organize great volume of work. Research ability. Meticulous attention to detail and infinite capacity for follow-through. Knowledge of publicity techniques. Some writing ability. Willingness to work long hours when necessary and under pressure.

Proofreader: Thorough working knowledge of English language and spelling. Familiarity with mechanics of printing, particularly composition. Knowledge of proofreading procedure. Some general editorial sense. Acquaintance with the standard reference books and knowledge of how to use them. College education or its equivalent.

Assistant in Charge of Credits to National Coordinating Director: Some college training desirable. Good, fast typing. Ability to handle correspondence and volume of detail under pressure. Experience in store selling, merchandising, store promotion quite beneficial. Otherwise, experience on staff in fashion or promotion work essential.

Correspondent for Promotion Department: Shorthand helpful, typing essential. Ability to handle correspondence, voluminous detail, the technical details of ordering blow-ups and reprints, answer inquiries on promotion from stores and manufacturers.

Reader Mail Supervisor: A merchandising background is helpful but not necessary. Should know the retail market. Research ability. Be able to compose and type letters.

METROPOLITAN NEWSPAPER

All that was said in the introduction to the publishing field, about the relation of the liberal arts curriculum to the commercial writing field, is especially true for newspaper work. No matter how specialized your college training may be, even to courses in the journalism school, you must be prepared to start with a routine job. There is nothing exciting about being a copygirl, an ad-taker, a typist or stenographer unless you realize the importance of learning the tools of this profession well.

The New York Times' requirements given below present the over-all approach of a metropolitan newspaper to prospective employees. Opportunities for advancement on the majority of large papers, however, are few. Your best policy is to be sure that you can meet these requirements and then see what the hometown or near-by small newspaper has to offer. Experience on a small daily or weekly is invaluable, because you will learn how a newspaper is published from its printing to delivery. Your duties may include everything from selling ads, writing personals and headlines, to helping with layouts and doing office work.

In your college work, concentrate on courses which will give you knowledge and understanding of current events—sociology, economics and political science. The journalism world is tough and competitive. The more practical your experience and education is, the better your chance will be of finding a place in it.

Employer: The New York Times.

Courses Needed: Liberal arts degree valued. An English major is helpful for a girl who wants to go into reporting. Whatever she has done in writing reports, letters or descriptions, or in creative writing, is excellent training. Her general associations with people, and her general social and intellectual maturity are also important.

Personality Requirements: Ability to state her qualifications in a direct, easy, comprehensive manner. She should know enough about business to be able to say how her qualifications might possibly serve the employer's needs. Ability to adjust to the temperaments of colleagues, to value others and herself. The following are very helpful: neatness, poise, friendliness, charm, ease of manner, good telephone voice, a business sense and a healthy respect for a time schedule.

Experience Valuable: Every work experience is valuable in that it contributes to the vocational maturity of the applicant. The applicant should know how to sell her own abilities. She should present a comprehensive résumé of her educational and vocational experiences.

Description of Work: Promotion on *The New York Times* is made within the organization, wherever possible. New workers, unless unusually qualified for a special department, begin as secretaries, stenographers, typists, ad-takers.

Minimum Skill Requirements: Secretary and stenographer should be a proficient speller, take dictation at 120 words per minute, type 50 words per minute, meet the personal qualifications noted above. Typist should be an excellent speller, meet personal qualifications noted above, type 50 words per minute. Ad-taker should be excellent speller, type 50 words per minute and meet personal qualifications noted above.

YOUR DISCOVERIES NOTED HERE

If printer's ink flows in your veins, you will be seeking out
some sort of print shop, or the editorial house connected with
it. Why not start with the school publication, your local newspaper; see where your talents might be used.

1. Name of Newspaper, Yearbook or Magazine:

2. Jobs Held:

3. Description of Work:

4. Over-all Evaluation of Experience:

TOOLS OF THE PROFESSIONS

Now add information which you have discovered about the publishing industry in general.

1. Names of Papers, Magazines, Book Publishers:

2. Employees Interviewed:

3. Job Titles:

4. Courses Needed:

5. Personality Requirements:

6. Experience Needed:

7. Background Reading:

Apparel Merchandising

Job Titles: Merchandise Director, Buyer, Fashion Director.

Employers: Department Stores, Specialty Shops, Manufacturers, Catalogue Houses.

Courses Needed: Every course in the liberal arts curriculum contributes to the essential skills needed in merchandising jobs. "A study of world fashions through the art and home economics departments," said one fashion director. "Psychology, or any subjects which help you to understand and get along with people—and mathematics and economics too, especially in the buying field," said another fashion director. "These seem vitally important to me."

Personality Requirements: Good health, this is a strenuous type of business. Enthusiasm. Leadership and ability to get along with people. Outgoing personality. Imagination and a flair for fashion, buying. Good taste, sound judgment.

Experience Needed: Sell—summers, weekends, during college, any time available. Many stores have training squads which particularly welcome the college graduate. Job titles leading up to the top merchandising positions are: salesclerk, head of stock, assistant buyer (sometimes associate buyer), buyer, merchandising counselor. If you have had experience in one or two of these beginning steps, and at graduation are still interested in the large merchandising occupations, you could enrich your undergraduate college training with courses related to your special product.

Description of Work: The merchandise director has the job of planning, guiding and directing buyers. The director controls the money spent, helps balance stocks and decides merchandising policy with the buyer and fashion director. The buyer plans her stocks, buys and directs the sale of merchandise. She must be a leader, know style and have good judgment as to what will sell in her particular store. She needs a mathematical mind so that she can plan stock intelligently, figure mark-ups, make a profit on what is bought.

The fashion director works with the buyer and merchandise manager, manufacturer or producer and the advertising department. The fashion director needs to have imagination, coupled with good judgment. She must be a leader in new ideas, know trends, be quick to sense and help develop them. The fashion director is a coordinator of related merchandise, right hats with right coats or suits, right shoes and bags, the proper color combinations.

Job Title: Fashion Promotion Director.

Employer: Cohama Fabrics, manufacturer and converter of woolens, silks, rayons.

Courses Needed: Writing, merchandising, publicity, fashion, fabrics, etc.

Personality Requirements: Sincere interest in all aspects of fashion; enthusiasm for meeting and working with people; some ability to write copy; a good imagination. A readiness to do almost any kind of job that will prepare you for promotion work.

Experience Needed: Any work in the fashion field.

Description of Work: To work on fabric promotions with retail stores and wholesale manufacturers in publicizing the trade name. To work on assembling new color cards, to name new colors. To work on fabric displays. To write promotion letters and copy for fashion releases.

YOUR DISCOVERIES NOTED HERE

The job descriptions just given were concerned only with apparel and fabrics. Merchandising operations, however, are necessary to every product in the world. What products interest you?

Experience in selling a product is the first step. If that start doesn't please you, and you feel (as what college girl has not?) that in your particular case, you have talents which will make a start somewhere nearer the top of the ladder possible, why not begin investigating, just for your information, at a merchandising business near your home or college? Interview the personnel manager at a manufacturing plant concerned with the product (food to fashions) which interests you:

1. Name of Plant:

2. Person Interviewed:

3. Experience Needed:

Summary Sheet for Social Sciences

Here is space for an over-all review and evaluation of the facts you have been accumulating—plus additional comments.

SCIENCES

The war upset the applecart in the science field, didn't it?
Or was it the end of hostilities? The applecart will always be
upset by growing knowledge, because new knowledge affects
every field in which men work. David Lilienthal said in
"Atomic Energy Is *Your* Business" (*New York Times Magazine*,
January 11, 1948):

*New knowledge inevitably brings changes. The atomic weapon
has changed the relation between nations and the problem of the
maintenance of peace. And atomic energy has brought changes
in the treatment of human suffering. . . . In agriculture the horizons
of new knowledge are practically unlimited. . . . It is fair to say that
the entire investment in the atomic energy project—now nearly
two and a half billion dollars—may be more than repaid by the
benefits to agriculture and to human nutrition alone.*

Every professional field imaginable comes within the orbit
of this power. You are still the same person, however, and
even though your imagination has been quickened, you should
choose to major and work in the science field because you
enjoy sustaining scientific interests throughout the rigorous
discipline required.

It is misleading, dangerously misleading, to relate any college course to any special occupation. In a variety of ways
this book has been saying that the liberal arts curriculum is
worth everything—or nothing—depending upon the individual. Some counselor may say quite sincerely that you really
should have a course in advanced organic chemistry for a
certain position, but that doesn't mean you'll get that position
by taking advanced organic. Recall *Mademoiselle's* specifications under the "Social Sciences": You will be disqualified if
you are *not* a competent stenographer. You will be disqualified if you are *only* a competent stenographer. A Bachelor's
degree in science is only the beginning, but that beginning is
vital and here are a few jobs open to you—at the beginning.
Large fields are mentioned, not courses.

Technology—All Fields

A technician's job can be simple or very complex, depending upon the area of research. Doctors' offices, hospital and commercial laboratories have one or more technicians. Sometimes the employer will teach you his particular techniques, if he judges you have become a dependable laboratory technician in those areas studied during college. Graduate work is essential for any duty beyond the simplest. What is your specialty? Medical? Physiological? Mathematical? Biological? Geographical? Geological? There is a laboratory needing your specialty in one or more of the following areas:

1. United States Civil Service Commission, Washington, D. C., and your state civil service.
2. State agricultural stations.
3. Institute of Animal Husbandry.
4. Bureau of Forestry.
5. Fish and Wildlife Service.
6. TVA projects and others.

For more detailed suggestions, check these two bulletins:

Industrial Research Laboratories of the United States, Bulletin 104; *Handbook of Scientific and Technical Societies and Institutions of the U.S.A. and Canada,* Bulletin 106. Published by the National Research Council, National Academy of Sciences, Washington, D. C. Many of the companies listed offer grants for research work.

YOUR DISCOVERIES NOTED HERE

1. What is my special interest, or interests, in the technician field? Biology? Mathematics? Geology?

2. What especially challenges, pleases, me most in this particular field? That is, why do I like it?

3. What do I plan to do about it?

Chemistry

Job Titles: Research Assistant, Senior Technician, Junior Technician.

Employers: Research Laboratory, Hospitals.

Courses Needed: A degree from a well-recognized college, with a major in chemistry is ideal; organic, inorganic, qualitative, quantitative chemistry are essential. Biology, zoology, physics majors may also qualify.

Personality Requirements: Those working in research must be willing to handle animals for experimental purposes, rats, mice, etc. Sometimes college girls are not willing to do this, but it is an important feature in a research laboratory. Patience to observe and record the minutest detail is also necessary.

Experience Needed: For junior technicians only, no experience is required if the candidate has had good science courses as noted above.

Description of Work: Research assistants and technicians are
engaged in research problems only. In the nonresearch
laboratories there are also research assistants, junior and
senior technicians, senior chemical technicians. The routine hospital analyses, blood count, urinanalysis, etc., are
done by a third group which has had special training.

YOUR DISCOVERIES NOTED HERE

1. For what job title can I qualify? Hospital laboratory,
   private laboratory, government agency?

You will be told that the industrial chemist is usually a man.
There are exceptions everywhere in the world, if you will
investigate. Write to:

1. The Women's Bureau for their *The Outlook for Women in
   Science,* Washington 25, D. C.
2. The American Chemical Society for their *Job Information
   on Vocational Guidance in Chemistry and Chemical Engineering,* 1155 - 16 Street N. W., Washington 6, D. C.

Ayers Directory mentioned on page 44 gives names and
addresses of chemical journals, which will suggest many
opportunities. Also, see page 93, the "Special Library Field."
Write your findings here.

Biological Sciences

Demand exceeds the number qualified for available positions in bacteriology. In women's favor, is the fact that some employers prefer them, believing they surpass men in tasks requiring close attention to detail, repetitious processes and in record-keeping. Women with undergraduate training find their chief sources of employment in hospitals and in state and city public health departments and laboratories. Those with a Ph. D. degree find their main outlet in teaching and research. . . .

According to estimates of the Botanical Society of America, by 1950 about 828 more botanists and 369 more plant pathologists will be needed than were available in 1946. . . . The new plant pathologists will be needed primarily for research. Two-thirds of the other newcomers are expected to go into teaching, still the chief outlet for women in botany. . . . Another outlet for women will be found in mycology, science of the fungi. In this recently expanded science, opportunities will be greatest for those who have a background in plant pathology, biochemistry and bacteriology.

Women general biologists, who outstrip other women in the biological sciences in the proportion they form (22.6 per cent) of the total employment in their branch of science, find their greatest opportunities in public health departments, hospitals, medical research centers, medical schools, high schools, colleges and universities. In college teaching, especially, the number of women biologists is expected to increase. . . . Other outlets for women biologists are such specialties as scientific illustration, writing, editing and library work. More women also will be employed in nature education in local communities. Courses in the applied fields of forestry and agriculture, as well as training in zoology and botany, will be helpful to women who aspire to this type of work.

Women in general zoology, less affected by the war than those in other sciences, will find openings similar in number and type to those available in the past. For the woman with the Bachelor degree, opportunities are chiefly in medical laboratory work, other medical or health work and high school teaching; for the woman Ph. D., they are in college teaching. An exception is the entomologist, whose greatest opportunities are in research work. Other likely avenues are scientific illustration, writing and editing.[9]

---

[9] From a news release, issued by the Women's Bureau, U. S. Department of Labor, September 1948 concerning *The Outlook for Women in the Biological Sciences*, Bulletin No. 223-3, the Women's Bureau, U. S. Department of Labor, Washington 25, D. C.

Job Title: Laboratory Technician (Medical Technologist is term often used in the medical field).

Employers: Hospitals, Private Doctors, Commercial Laboratories, Public Health Centers.

Courses Needed: At least two years of college chemistry, preferably three or four. A real interest in the biological sciences as evidenced by the choice in college of biology courses, or see "experience" paragraph.

Personality Requirements: Patience, capacity for detail, willingness to work long hours, to stand on your feet, to handle small animals for experimental purposes and to endure unpleasant odors. Pleasant telephone voice. Ability to get along with people. Poise. Legible handwriting essential, also good general health and good eyesight.

Experience Valuable: Sometimes a private physician will teach a promising applicant the basic skills such as blood count, urinanalysis, etc. These also are taught in most college physiology laboratory courses. Summer employment in a local physician's office or hospital laboratory will help the student know her own capacities for further study, and strengthen her employment opportunities after college.

Description of Work: Duties differ, depending upon the type of institution in which you are working. Basic ones are performing blood count, analyzing urine, routine chemical analyses of blood and other body fluids, routine bacteriology, operating electrocardiagraph machine. This last operation is not a basic part of the average technologist's duties. It may be necessary in one of the smaller hospitals or in some doctors' offices, but is an added accomplishment, like X-ray, rather than a fundamental necessity.

Job Title: Nursing.

The need for nurses is urgent enough to warrant consideration at least, by every college girl. Your response may be a ready one, on first thought. But have you ever really thoughtfully considered the nursing profession—considered its whole gamut of opportunities—from bedside nurse in a hospital, private duty specialist, public health education, and private duty nurses, to instructor in a nursing school or director of nursing?

All schools have standards for admission. Your eligibility to enter college is determined by high school grades or the college board examination grades. Schools of nursing are first governed by academic record, and preference is given to those who have shown ability and achievement. Psychometric tests are also a part of the admission requirement in the better schools.

Nursing schools' pre-admission tests which measure science information, reading speed, arithmetic reasoning and such, are probably not of so much interest to you, since the tests are geared for less than college level, as is the test which purports to measure your degree of self-sufficiency, dominance, emotional stability and extraversion (the Bernreuter Personality Inventory). The picture all these measurements together present to the admission's officers at a nursing school tells them about your probable success in the profession. No tests ever say you must take this course, must enter this profession, but tests are helpful indicators of your probable success in the school employing them.

Leaders in the field are eager for prospective applicants to begin early in high school, early in college, to learn the requirements of various nursing schools. There are two types of nursing schools of special interest to the girl attending college: the university nursing school which requires a college degree for admission; and the collegiate schools which are affiliated with colleges or universities and offer a combined nursing and academic program of four to five years. There is a great deal to be learned about schools suited to your own needs. If this field interests you at all, follow through on as many of these suggestions as seem appropriate.

1. Visit at least three different types of nursing schools—
   hospital, collegiate, university. Be sure to read *Nursing for
   the Future,* by Esther Lucile Brown (Russell Sage Foundation, New York, 1948). As a study of nursing as it is prac-
   ticed today and an evaluation of its future, it particularly
   affects the college girl interested in the profession.

2. Become acquainted with the *American Journal of Nursing.*
   The library undoubtedly has it.

3. Write to the Nursing Information Bureau, 1790 Broadway,
   New York, N. Y., for information about the proper school
   for you, considering your needs, financial, educational, etc.

4. Keep a record of your feelings about this as a career—
   semester by semester, if you like. Your reasons may be
   very undignified, even sound silly, but that is all right.
   When the director of nursing asks why you are interested
   in the nursing profession you may say, "I wish to serve
   humanity," or some equally acceptable reply. That may
   well be very true at a maturer age, even though your first
   why (you secretly know) was . . . . . I liked the uniform!

Freshman Year ....Why?

Sophomore Year ....Why?

Junior Year ....Why?

Senior Year   ....Why?

5. Which is the best school for you? Collegiate? University?

6. Why?

7. Have you any questions to ask the National League for Nursing Education, 1790 Broadway, New York, N. Y., about college courses, financing your nursing training, selection of a nursing school?

8. Make a note of the hospitals visited and any conferences you may have with the director of training.

9. The career of occupational therapist is related to nursing. Write The American Occupational Therapy Association, 33 West 42nd Street, New York, N. Y., for information.

Job Title: Aquatic Biologist.

Employer: U. S. Fish and Wildlife Service.

Courses Needed: A.B. degree is sufficient for a technician. Research biologist needs at least a Master's degree; a Doctor's degree is even more helpful in obtaining a job.

The research biologist should study related sciences that will prepare her to pry into the secrets of life. Some related subjects that will prepare her for modern biological research are: chemistry, especially biochemistry; sufficient mathematics to understand statistical methods of analysis; enough physics to be able to adapt electrical and mechanical devices to a specific problem.

Personality Requirements: Integrity. Adaptability. Initiative. Persistence. Ability to get along well with coworkers. Ability to take advantage of constructive criticism without resentment. Curiosity, a desire to know why animals react to stimuli as they do.

Experience Valuable: Biological aide in government laboratory, carrying on work in which student is particularly interested, such as, Fish and Wildlife Service, Bureau of Animal Husbandry, Bureau of Forestry, etc. Laboratory assistant in department of zoology at a large university. Assistant to research biologist doing field work at one of the marine biological laboratories, most of which are operated by universities.

YOUR DISCOVERIES NOTED HERE

Mathematics and Statistics

Mathematics is an ubiquitous tool, omnipresent in the research laboratory and business. It might be easier to find organizations which are not employing mathematicians than to specify those which do. The world of finance offers the college girl with a mathematical mind, or at least one who can say, "I am not afraid of figures," many opportunities (see "Tools of Business").

The majority of women mathematicians with degrees are, as in pre-war days, engaged in teaching, or hold jobs with insurance and other business firms. Because men appear to be leaving high school teaching, it will become increasingly important for women, particularly for those who are able to teach physics or chemistry along with mathematics. . . . For the girl who takes her Ph.D. degree, teaching also will be the usual opportunity, though in her case it probably will be in a college or university. . . . In 1946 the American Mathematical Society found that there were not enough well-trained women to fill the first-class mathematical jobs open to them in colleges and universities.

Unlike mathematicians, statisticians find their greatest opportunities not in the classroom but in industry and government, both federal and state. Among state agencies in which women are employed are departments of labor, public welfare and health. . . . Though accelerated by the wartime use of statistics in control work and planning, the increase in statistical opportunities first started about ten years ago. The growth in recent years, according to the National Research Council, has been especially great in the fields of (1) industrial statistics, quality control, research and development; (2) research in biological sciences; (3) collection and analysis of government statistics; (4) market research and commercial sample surveys; and (5) psychological testing. . . . For at least a few years to come, opportunity will be ample for statistically trained women and they will not encounter as much discrimination in this relatively new and growing field as women in many other professional fields have had to combat. Moreover, a shortage of statisticians at the Bachelor's as well as the Ph. D. level is expected to continue for some time.[10]

---

[10]From a news release issued by the Women's Bureau, U. S. Department of Labor, August 1948, concerning *The Outlook for Women in Mathematics and Statistics* (one of an over-all series on *The Outlook for Women in Science*). The Women's Bureau, U. S. Department of Labor, Washington 25, D. C.

Here are some other specific examples of requirements and opportunities.

New York Stock Exchange: Statistician. Advanced statistical training, ability to make analyses.

Chartist. Ability to make charts and use calculating machines. Samples of charts applicant has made are always studied with interest.

Esso Standard Oil Company: Mathematician. We prize the mathematically trained college girl. She does not need to have a full mathematics major (particularly if she also has secretarial skills). We seldom employ women as chemists, but we do value a chemistry major.

Economist. Market research, employee relations research, economic study and the supply section of our supply and transportation department use both economic and business administration majors occasionally. In most cases, however, it is desirable for the employee to be a competent typist.

Researcher. We do not use women in chemical research in the headquarters office.

Job Titles: Typists, Secretaries, Machine Operators, Statisticians, Interviewers, Analysis Clerks.

Employers: Advertising Agencies, Public Opinion Poll Takers, Organizations or Departments in Manufacturing Plants (consumer goods in particular) and in Retail Stores.

Courses Needed: The whole liberal arts curriculum, or that of any college, business or technical school.

Description of Personality Requirements and Work (from the Gallup Poll office, American Institute of Public Opinion, Princeton, New Jersey):

Typist. Must have average proficiency.

Secretaries. Must have average proficiency.

International Business Machine Operators. Must be able to operate the card punch and card sorting machines. The college girl interested in machine operations at all will want to learn how to wire the IBM board for its many intricate calculations.

Statisticians. Use of slide rule, working knowledge of elementary statistics.

Editorial Assistants. Liberal arts degree.

Interviewers. We use a large number of women (usually young college-graduate housewives), as part-time interviewers throughout the United States. As a rule, surveys are sent out about twice a month. This activity appeals to the married woman who doesn't want a full-time position, but wants to be doing something to stimulate her interest in people and current affairs. (Contact Public Opinion Surveys, Inc., 16 Chambers Street, Princeton, New Jersey.)

Analysis Clerks. Women are used in ballot work. Women with training in journalism, psychology, sociology can qualify for these positions.

YOUR DISCOVERIES NOTED HERE

During your college life what have you done of a statistical nature?

1. Did you take part in a census-taking project? In interpreting the data gathered? (Keep the actual study.)

2. Investigate any community; there is a job there if you want it. Be sure to discover what type of statistician you are: Are you satisfied to do the problem at hand, or do you always want to go beyond the problem to discover how it relates to a whole situation? Insurance firms and banks need both types.

3. What in mathematics interests you most — teaching, research, commerce?

Summary Sheet for Sciences

Here is space for an over-all review and evaluation of the facts already accumulated—plus additional comments.

HUMANITIES

In your lifetime, or your children's, the world will push research in the humanities and social sciences to a point equaling the progress made in harnessing the forces of nature. Consequently every occupation either belongs in the humanities section or is affected by it. This is a point to keep clearly before you as we discuss a few of the jobs which come to mind easily when a girl, having majored in a subject assigned to the "humanities" group, says, "I want to do something in my major field."

Religious Education

Job Titles:

General. Director of Religious Education, Educational Director, Minister of Religious Education.

Specialized. Director of Children's Work, Director of Youth Work, Director of Adult Work, College Student Secretary.

Employers: Churches and Synagogues, Schools and Colleges, Local, District, State and National Denominational Agencies and Councils of Churches.

Courses Needed: Broad liberal arts background (preferably including courses in religion, the Bible, philosophy, psychology and education) is the best preparation; training on a graduate level, such as is offered by various schools of religious education and theological seminaries is desirable (and is being increasingly required by certain denominations).

Personality Requirements: An emotionally mature person, with a growing religious experience, interested in and able to work with others.

Experience Helpful: Volunteer work of all kinds in a local church; working with groups in various agencies; counselor in summer camp; active participation in church groups, YWCA, interfaith groups, etc. on the campus.

Description of Work (from The Pioneer Valley Religious Education Association, Springfield, Massachusetts):

Through role as administrator, interpreter and executor of the local church's educational program to fulfill such varied functions as: (1) the recruiting and supervision of group leaders; (2) the guidance of both worship and service programs in which children, teen-agers and young adults participate; (3) the organization and leadership of study programs for all age groups; (4) interpretation to the community at large of the place of religious education in that community's life; (5) personal counseling of program constituents.

Background Reading:

Shaver, Erwin L., *Directors of Religious Education—A Survey,* pamphlet, 1947. Order from the author, 14 Beacon Street, Boston 8, Massachusetts.

Harner, Nevin C., *The Educational Work of the Church.* Abingdon-Cokesbury Press, 1939.

YOUR DISCOVERIES NOTED HERE

Look for increased employment in this field. Churches are becoming aware of their opportunities for wider usefulness in meeting community needs through services such as nursery schools, counseling for teen-agers and adults. Pick the church you are interested in, find out what it plans to do in the area of community relationships. Also write to the Federal Council of Churches of Christ in America, 297 Fourth Avenue, New York, N. Y., for current information about student delegates to the Ecumenical Institute at Celigny near Geneva, Switzerland, where men and women theological students prepare for service under the auspices of the World Council of Churches. This is something to plan for.

1. Name of Church:

2. Employee Interviewed:

3. Counselors Employed by This Church:

4. Courses Needed for These Duties:

5. Personality Requirements:

6. Background Reading:

Special Library Field

Job Titles: Researchers, Research Analysts, Information
Specialists.

Possible Employers: Advertising Agencies, Medical or Phar-
maceutical Concerns, Industrial and Business Corporations, Geography and Map Departments, Nursing Schools
and Hospitals, Historical and Fine Arts Collections,
Museums, Newspapers and Magazines, Social Science
Organizations, Radio Companies, Transportation Companies, Insurance Companies, Law Firms, Religious
Organizations, Motion Picture Companies.

Courses Needed: A.B. or B.S. in any field of interest to the
student. Degree from a library school. An interest in
some specific subject in which she would like to work.
The biggest demand right now is, of course, for science
graduates. Chemical and other scientific firms engaged
in the study of electronics, radar, atomic energy, etc. are
asking for trained technical librarians. A reading knowledge of at least one foreign language is always helpful.
French, scientific German, and Russian are called for.
Scientific German is almost an essential skill.

Personality Requirements: Ability to work under pressure to
meet deadlines, to sense what is new. You must be able
to supplement technical training in unearthing the essential facts the employer requires, facts which are sometimes
in many languages.

Experience Valuable: Summer work in a special library or
library work during college. With this as an undergraduate background, it is frequently possible for the
recent college graduate to work in a special library and
take graduate courses in library science in the evening.

Your Discoveries Noted Here

This one will be easy. Why not check with the college library
staff? Find out what training and experience are represented,

what special talents and skills are displayed by the staff members. You have a hometown library. What are the professional qualifications represented there? Write to the Executive Secretary, Special Libraries Association, 31 East 10th Street, New York, N. Y., for information about its chapter in your locality. Or, ask the manager of any institution which attracts your interest, for any reason at all, if a trained librarian is on his staff, if not, who takes care of their information, books, correspondence, files? It's quite a profession.

1. Name of Institution:

2. Employee Interviewed:

3. Job Titles:

4. Courses Needed:

5. Personality Requirements:

United Nations

Employer: UN Personnel Office, Lake Success, New York.

Job Titles: Trainee Posts—Junior Professional, Junior Administrative.

There are a limited number of these positions open for American citizens, as there is at present a disproportionate representation from the U.S.A. Representatives from foreign member nations are ideally suited for positions in the trainee area. These fall in the broad field of social sciences. Requirements are based upon intelligence, education, general aptitude together with, if possible, a knowledge of both of the working languages (French and English), or one working language and one of the five official languages, Chinese, French, Russian, Spanish and English.

Translator and Interpreter Posts: Candidates for these posts must pass competitive examinations, must have an excellent command of two of the official languages. Knowledge of a third official language is highly desirable.

Clerical and Stenographic Openings: These continue to occur more frequently than those in other fields and will probably be filled, in good percentage with recruits from this country. Service in a secretarial post is not recommended for apprenticeship for a professional career in the United Nations. Candidates for these posts must pass competitive examinations. The present speed requirement in dictation

for senior stenographers is 96 words per minute and for
junior stenographers, 80 words per minute. A typing
speed of 40 to 60 words per minute is required. Verbatim
reporters must have a speed of 180 to 200 words per
minute.

General Comments: Staff requirements change from time to
time, and it is impossible to predict the needs. The best
general advice is to follow the ordinary college courses,
perhaps with a bias toward languages or political science,
and to follow with interest the events in the international field. Trainee positions are continually developing. Occasional inquiries made at the personnel office will
keep you informed of the most recent developments.

Foreign Countries

Beg, borrow, or earn the money for a pleasure trip if you
think a job abroad is a glamourous undertaking. Employment
abroad is arduous, lonesome, and at times uncomfortable. If
your interest survives this preliminary survey, maybe you really
do want "something abroad." Here are some sources of
information about the opportunities.

Office of International and Cultural Affairs, State Department,
Washington, D. C.: Secretaries and other office-skilled
workers needed. Fluency in Spanish, Portuguese and
English demanded in addition to competency in an office
skill.

Experts. Economists (tariff, foreign exchange, etc.);
geologists (for that special section); nurses, doctors, etc.

Office of Education, Division of International Educational
Relations, Washington, D. C.: Write to Dr. Kenneth Hol-
land, President, Inter-American Educational Foundation,
regarding need for teachers, group workers.

Council for Inter-American Cooperation, 57 William Street,
New York 5, N. Y. Write for general information regarding current needs for general workers.

The Travel Agent

Chasing springtime around the world—that was the travel agent's job before the war; it flourished in the Traveling Twenties, say from 1922 to 1929. It is coming back.

Thomas Cook[11] and "Ask Mr. Foster"[12] maintain training schools for their agents. Traveled war veterans, of course, have preference for these tasks, but college women need not despair. Thought and planning, some careful budgeting, too, provide the opportunity you need. If you can take a trip, one of the "packaged" trips will do. Note every service along the way: how hotel accommodations were made; how recreation was planned; how transportation was arranged. Become acquainted with the complete setup and those in charge.

A second, very effective stage, with or without having experienced the trip itself, is to sell trips to your fellow students, family, neighbors. There is usually a travel agent on every college campus—why not you?

Your Discoveries Noted Here

Here is a summary sheet for your special notations:

1. Are you a linguist? What languages could you use as a stenotype operator, for example?

---

[11]Thomas Cook and Sons, Inc., 587 Fifth Avenue, New York, N. Y.
[12]"Ask Mr. Foster" Travel Service, Inc., 30 Rockefeller Plaza, New York, N. Y.

2. How about graduate work, in a specialty useful to international organizations? Does your college affiliate with a Washington, D. C., public service training institution? Your dean will know.

3. What selling ideas can you suggest to your favorite travel agency?

Air Transportation

Employer: American Airlines.

This office has literature which will be sent upon request, or you might find it in the college library.[13] There may be an airline representative on campus, selling trips and giving information. Whatever airline you investigate, there will be jobs for women, similar to these outlined by American Airlines.

---

[13]Personnel offices are located in principal cities throughout the United States. Personnel Director, American Airlines, 122 East 42nd Street, New York, N. Y.

Ticket and Reservations Clerks: Chosen for their pleasing voices, education, poise, appearance and personality; they are given in-service training during which they are under close supervision. Geography, English, public speaking, psychology and languages are suggested preparatory courses. Usually airlines ask that applicants be twenty-one or older. They must have had at least two years of college, or be high school graduates with two years of appropriate sales or business training.

Stewardesses: A stewardess, generally speaking, must be from 21 to 28 years of age, weigh from 100 to 125 pounds, be somewhere between 5 feet, and 5 feet, 6 inches in height and able to pass the flight physical examination. She must be unmarried, and usually cannot keep her job after marriage. The ability to wear a uniform with distinction and maintain an attractive appearance, to show a friendly interest in people and to deal with them skillfully is a very important qualification that rates high. Psychology, physiology, first aid, music, art, current events, geography, physical education are suggested preparatory courses.

Junior Teletype Operators: Teletypes are used for communication between ground bases. They are also used by the radiotelephone operator. The teletype operator, who may be either a man or woman, reads teletype tape at a speed of 10 words a minute, punches tape at 60 words a minute, and operates the teletype on the direct keyboard at 40 words a minute. Besides knowing how to operate the machine, the operator must know the regulations pertaining to his work and general operations procedure.

Radiotelephone and Radiotelegraph Operators: Require specialized training. There are many radio and aeronautical schools in the United States that give the training that will enable a young man or woman to obtain an FCC license. Physics is the most important college subject. Algebra, geometry, trigonometry, English, spelling and typewriting are essential.

Junior Clerk and Typist, Secretary: See pages 30, 34.

Machine Operator: Because of the rapid expansion of business, the airline industry has kept pace with other industries in doing as much of its accounting work by machines as is practicable. These machines include "punch card" equipment, adding machines, comptometers, bookkeeping and calculating machines. The operation of these machines can be learned in a relatively short time, but they require alert, active people to operate them correctly and without errors. Some business machine companies have training schools for operators. The industry generally engages operators from these schools (see IBM, p. 87). In some instances from these schools inexperienced people who acquire training on the job.

Meteorologists: The men and women employed by the airlines to study atmospheric conditions and forecast the weather are meteorologists. They have had engineering and mathematical training, plus specialized training. The responsibility of a meteorologist's job is such that he must have good judgment, perception and the capacity for sound reasoning. Meteorologists do not necessarily work the customary shifts. Their shift schedule is usually determined by the flight frequency at their base. College major in physics, advanced mathematics and two years of a physical science are essential. Physical geography or physiography, freehand drawing, languages are helpful. Typing is helpful, but not essential.

YOUR DISCOVERIES NOTED HERE

1. What qualifications do you have for what job title?

2. What job titles of a similar nature have you discovered on
   your own explorations?

3. What will you do about them?

Museums

The world is full of museums. What is your special interest?
There is a museum, or department of a museum, concerned
with it. Below are the job titles for which the Metropolitan
Museum employs college girls. Where do you fit? The museum of your interest, not necessarily the Metropolitan, has
employment opportunities in similar categories.

Employer: Metropolitan Museum of Art, New York City.

Stenographer: Each department in the museum has at least one. We prefer a college graduate for the curatorial departments, but a full degree is not essential. We like (who doesn't) what is generally known as the "college type," alert, well groomed, friendly. But the only rigid qualification is that she be a good stenographer (100-120 words per minute, dictation; 60 words per minute, typing).

Typist: We employ no one for "clerical work." A typist (60 words per minute) can do all the duties generally known as clerical. Most of our typists are not college graduates.

Librarian: This is a large department with the Metropolitan. A college degree (any major, but one in fine arts is preferred) plus a degree in library science is essential. A reading fluency in at least one foreign language is invaluable. German is, almost, an essential tool. The interest in fine arts might have been acquired, not through college study but on an avocational basis, if accompanied by the library science degree and language fluency.

Artist: College girls are employed in the Exhibition Department as artists; they must be able to do some architectural drawing, model making, craft work. Their abilities and interests are very specialized. This is a very small department in the largest art museum in the U.S.A. The Metropolitan employs three artists: the head of the department and two young women, one of whom is a typist, who also takes care of the office routine. There are very few openings here.

Business Department Employees: Here the Museum employs the usual staff of office workers: stenographer, typist (as noted above), bookkeeper, bookkeeping machine operator. A college degree is not required. Promotion is on the basis of skill and within the department.

Education Department Employee Guide: College girl, history of art, Bachelor degree in fine arts, or some special qualification for a certain curatorial department, who also has had student teacher-training experience, or some group leadership activity; also someone who is taking, or wishes to do advanced study in the fine arts field, who is friendly, speaks well and easily to strangers, makes a pleasing appearance, is enthusiastic about her work.

Curatorial Department Employees: The Metropolitan has the following departments, the titles of which indicate the specialization required for advancement within the department: Department of Conservation and Technical Research in Egyptian Art, Greek and Roman Art, Near Eastern Art, Far Eastern Art, Mediaeval Art and the Cloisters, Renaissance and Modern Art, the American Wing, Paintings, Prints, Arms and Armor.

In each of these departments, there may be found, depending upon the size of the collection and the work to be done in the field represented, the following job titles, from lowest rank to highest: Research Fellow, Assistant Curators, Senior Research Fellow, Associate Curator, Curator. Applicants with advanced degrees or experience in a smaller museum, who wish to specialize in a particular department, represent various degrees of accomplishment in the special field of knowledge. There are very few openings in this department and for that reason, when one does occur, it is difficult to find applicants who have had the training and experience needed.

Information Desk Attendants: Beginning workers, college girls, are hired for duty here. Primary requirements are a "sales personality," interest and knowledge of fine arts, a liking for all types of people.

Photographic Department: Only large museums have such a department as a permanent part of their staffs. Without doubt such an applicant would have been a camera club enthusiast and have samples of her work to show.

Retouching Department: A chemistry major, one interested especially in matching colors, mixing paints, could, theoretically, qualify here. No woman has, as yet, ever been employed.

Editorial Department: Beginning positions here for the college girl would be either as a secretary or as a skilled ediphone operator. Either one would have to be skilled in using libraries to check facts. Everyone in the editorial department types. English majors are preferred, but a girl from another major, with editorial experience or qualifications, would certainly be considered.

The Catalogue Department: Everything which comes into the museum is described in words and by photograph on a record card. The object's history is documented. The Metropolitan in New York City employs seven persons in this department: a superior, chief cataloguer, a senior cataloguer, three junior cataloguers and a clerk-typist. These researchers are young people who are resourceful in digging up information, who find it easy to talk to people, to get facts from books or from busy experts. Personable, resourceful, quick-minded, young college girls.

YOUR DISCOVERIES NOTED HERE

What job titles have you discovered of interest to you in your own museum search?

Radio

Everywhere you hear that radio jobs, the exciting kind, aren't open, that the comparatively small staff now on hand never die, never resign, and expansion in service is a matter of adding equipment, not hiring more employees. This is true. But you know there are openings, not in the large cities probably, but better still in your home town or its neighbor.

Read the trade magazines, *Variety, Tune In, The Billboard, Radio Daily.* You must know what's going on.

Employer: National Broadcasting Company, Inc. (See also pages 33, 36.)

Dramatic Work: Office work and dramatic work are entirely separate. Anyone wishing an audition should write to the Auditions Section of the Program Department, giving qualifications and experience. When auditions are unusually heavy, appointments are sometimes limited to people with experience only. Each case is individual and a date is usually set quite far in advance.

While the local stations have the same needs as the extensive network operations of the National Broadcasting Company, their departments are frequently combined, thus requiring employees who are jacks-of-all-trades. Consequently, the hurdles between specific duties in the basic departments— engineering, programming, business management, marketing and public relations—will be lower in the small station than in the large. On the other hand, the networks, because of their extensive departmentalization, require specialists. NBC says in *Job Opportunities:*

If your goal is a job as an announcer, production director, salesman, or script writer, the quickest and best route from school to a network post is usually via the local stations which are not owned and operated by the networks. There, because the operation is smaller and the requirements for specialization are not so great, you have an opportunity to get broad experience. In accounting, research, personnel, engineering and junior administrative jobs the broad background in radio is not quite so necessary and it becomes easier to gain within a network the experience needed in such jobs.

YOUR DISCOVERIES NOTED HERE

Here you list the local radio station and its job titles with
minimum requirements for each. If you do this while in college, you will be familiar with the field and the personnel in
it before leaving college.

1. Name of Station:

2. Employee Interviewed:

3. Job Titles at This Particular Station:

4. Minimum Skills Required:

5. What Courses Are Helpful:

Motion Picture Industry

There are three divisions of employment in this industry: the commercial, editorial and technical. The technical jobs have one door of entrance, the technical school; the other jobs can be approached in as many ways as your ingenuity allows.

COMMERCIAL

Job Titles: Secretaries, Typists, Clerks, Accounts Receivable Clerks, Teletype Operators.

Employer: Metro-Goldwyn-Mayer.

Courses Needed: We care only for the applicant's ability to do her particular job. Competency tests are given for stenography and typing jobs. Promotion is confined to the department in which the girl is working. There is no relation between skill acquired in the commercial division and that used in the editorial.

General Information: We have thirty-one major offices throughout the United States. If a girl wants to get acquainted with our firm, she might try for a commercial job near at home. Editorial work, which most college girls want, is done either in New York or in Hollywood. Editorial work is built on editorial experience in motion pictures.

EDITORIAL

Job Titles: Editors, Assistants, Researchers, Rewrite, all broken down into special categories. (For example, a researcher is one who can or has specialized in such areas as research on shoes, interiors, titles, legal regulations, costumes.)

Employer: Twentieth Century-Fox Corporation.

Courses Needed: Every course in the whole world is valuable, depending upon the special interest of the applicant. (Also, refer to section on "Publishing.")

There are hundreds of smaller firms, in addition to such large ones as Twentieth Century-Fox, producing educational, industrial, advertising films, where beginners start and are trained in their special requirements. Here breadth of ability is appreciated and one particular specialty is a necessity. See how many firms you can discover in the locality in which you wish to work, which sell goodwill, advertising, public relations by film production. The U. S. State Department and Department of Agriculture also have staffs of motion picture technicians, such as foreign language experts, production technicians, editors, etc. A composite of the skills used by small firms, organizations and government agencies is as follows:

Secretary: Good secretarial skill is the first essential. The more interest she has in the moving picture business, the more she will learn—to write titles, print the titles written by others, do editorial work in general, proofread, copy, check copy, etc.

Librarian: Researcher. A library science degree, always good, will not be required, merely skill in using libraries, in finding information, finding pictures. This librarian might even have ideas for scripts along the special line represented by her firm. For example, an automobile tire manufacturer might employ, under the heading of advertising, a movie firm to take pictures of roads throughout the country. The girl, acting as "researcher" might easily present ideas for such a script. Versatility is essential in the small-type motion picture company.

Bookkeeper: One script writer in a small organization got her start as a bookkeeper-accountant, wrote scripts on the side. Remember, this would *never* happen in a large house—well, hardly ever.

See the trade publication, *Film News,* 15 West 38th Street, New York, N. Y., for names of producers small enough to use beginners such as:

1. Motion Picture Producers and Distributors of America, Inc., 28 West 44th Street, New York, N. Y.
2. Encyclopedia Britannica Films, 1150 Wilmett Avenue, Wilmett, Illinois. The vice-president in charge of research

says they employ recent college graduates who have had "strong majors in the natural and social sciences, language, and arts as junior research assistants."

3. International Film Foundation, 1600 Broadway, New York, N. Y.

4. William Ganz Co., 40 East 49th Street, New York, N. Y.

5. Filmcraft, 2826 Decatur Avenue, Bronx, New York, N. Y.

6. Large advertising agencies in New York City, Los Angeles, Detroit, Chicago.

Innovations in Hollywood (or New York) come from general acquaintance and an inquisitive mind. You poke around— see what you can find and what you can make of it. Here are some job titles to keep in mind when you are hunting around.

Costume Designer: Sketching ability plus wide and growing knowledge of all periods in history. Studios are in touch with commercial art schools, or go on your own with samples and a sales talk.

Writers: Write, write, write. Start anywhere, and keep your eye on a goal.

Music Cutter: Ability to read and hear music with accuracy. Experience in small firms with the problems involved in cutting, splicing and editing films.

Business Manager of Studio's Music Department: Combination of business skills (bookkeeping, cost accounting), musical ability and appreciation, plus knowledge of union regulations—quite a combination of talents.

YOUR DISCOVERIES NOTED HERE

Designing

Job Title: Fashion Designing.

Employers: Clothing Manufacturers, Designing Establishments.

Courses Needed: Art courses by the basketful and ability to draw from life—say a little better than "fairly well." The home economics department will also have valuable courses. Granted the basic ability to "think and draw around the think," a designer needs background. Designing is 5 per cent talent and 95 per cent hard work founded upon experience. Unless you are the rare genius who is born with 95 per cent talent, you will need association with the world of ideas and people, not just design school training on top of a high school education.

Personality Requirements: Appreciation of the personal worth of individuals, a love of color, of line, self-confidence born of self-knowledge. Willingness to work.

Experience Valuable: Any work with materials. If you have enthusiasm for this kind of work, your natural instincts will lead you to try your hand at a number of things, which will total up in an experience column, such as costume designing for high school and college plays or community activities. Do you make your own clothes, those of a sister or mother?

Description of Work: To create designs for new dresses, put new ideas for clothes into picture form so that new patterns may be made from them. Designs must be especially adapted for one age group. Designers these days are divided into specialties.

Background Reading: Williams, Beryl, *Fashion Is Our Business.* J. P. Lippincott, New York, 1945.
"Little Cutters." *Fortune Magazine,* May 1945.

YOUR DISCOVERIES NOTED HERE

Art

The artist uses her skill either as a supporting role for another profession or as the principal actress. Whichever you choose, the art world is highly competitive, depending as it does on both tangible and intangible skills. You will need to be confident, well-trained and highly imaginative to succeed.

Job Titles: Paste-up Girl, Layout Artist, Letterer, Photo Retoucher, Photographer, Magazine Illustrator, Cartoonist, Industrial Designer, Display and Package Designer, Book Designer, Magazine Production Manager.

Employers: Advertising Agencies, Publishers, Museums, Schools, Social Work Agencies, Display Designing Companies, Photographers, Publicity and Public Relations Departments, Art Dealers, Cartographers, Film Companies, Architects. (To start you thinking along highways not so widely traveled, here is one very specialized art area —cartography. C. S. Hammond & Company hires college

women specializing in geography as assistants to research cartographers to trace maps, index, proofread and
check facts. Drafting, secretarial or librarian training are
not required for those jobs but are considered valuable,
along with a knowledge of research methods. Those hired
for actual map-drafting positions are not required to have
a college background but previous drafting experience is
a "must." Coloring, lettering and layout skills count for
little, but drafting and a thorough knowledge of map
reproduction techniques are all-important.)

Courses Needed: For the majority of these specialties you will
need commercial art courses. Since many art schools have
evening classes, your business tools can be used to finance
this specialized training. If, however, you know the field
in which you want to use a palette and brush, it would be
wise to take courses that will familiarize you with its problems and functions.

YOUR DISCOVERIES NOTED HERE

In an effort to put a foundation under those dreams ask yourself some questions.

1. For which specialty do I have talent? Illustrations, layout,
   lettering, photography?

2. When can I take a commercial art course? While in school,
   on vacation or after graduation?

3. How can I afford it? What "something else" skills do I have to use?

4. Memo of personal investigations in the art world.

Musicology

There are many similarities between the field of music and that of art. For one thing the choice is whether to be a performing musician or to use your musical knowledge as a specialty in some other area of work. There is, for example, a tremendous need for musically trained employees in schools, social work agencies, public recreation programs, various aspects of therapeutic treatment, special libraries and religious education. Also, as in art, you need specific courses plus general knowledge of any special area in which musical ability can be used. Since music publishing is one of the less publicized sides of the music world, let's use it as a sample of how this particular world can be explored.

MUSIC PUBLISHING

Music publishers have not been very hospitable to the woman musicologist in beginning jobs. Two of the large commercial houses say, "We use only men as proofreaders and arrangers. A woman must be an expert in her field, a performing artist, educator or musicologist to interest us except in the well-known business capacities of secretary, bookkeeper, saleswoman."

Employer: Silver Burdett Company Textbook Publishers. As the textbook field has its own technicalities, a prerequisite for the position of saleswoman or editor in the music field is actual and successful classroom experience. This background is combined with some secretarial or clerical experience prior to representing the company. Every editor is a college graduate. (Another large publishing house, a leader in the audio-visual education field says: "We can easily secure learned musicologists and excellent musical technicians. The need is for people who know how to apply this specialized knowledge to the curriculum. General education plus specialized knowledge must include practical experience in transmitting this to the student at successive levels.")

YOUR DISCOVERIES NOTED HERE

All businesses have established prerequisites which certainly are to be respected and used as guides. But do you have a new idea? Try it out at home, school or on friends. Then approach the large companies with proof that the idea works, can be sold.

1. What is your dream?

2. Where can you experiment with it? What would be the results?

Summary Sheet for Humanities

Here is space for an over-all review and evaluation of the facts you have been accumulating—plus additional comments.

SPACE FOR THE JOB THAT CAN'T BE CLASSIFIED

New jobs seem to spring up over night. New jobs grow; like everything else, sometimes the growth is so fast as to seem spontaneous. Here is a fact well tested by experience: If you choose your major on the basis of your intellectual interests, you will be able—if indeed you could at any time have been able—to learn quickly the basic skills of the new work. If you choose a specialization on the basis of vocational choice alone, you are just missing more fun than anyone has a right to miss in college. Furthermore, your vocational choice may change with every wind of industry and no solid development of personality or interest will have been achieved.

This workbook does not pretend to give a complete analysis of the vocational world. It merely hopes to get you started. So here is space for an additional vocation which has suggested itself. Investigate, become a researcher on requirements; if, after learning the requirements, you are still enthusiastic won't that tell you something about yourself?

1. Job Title:

2. Employer:

3. Courses Helpful or Essential:

4. Personality Requirements:

5. Description of Work:

6. Background Reading:

Job Specification Summary

If you have been gathering your own specifications along with those given in Chapters III, IV and V, you will be impatient with any summary except the one you are eager to write yourself. Certainly you have heard at every interview that the employer expects—takes for granted that it will be found—in fact, demands that the liberal arts college send him only those applicants whose personalities have been educated along with their minds! College majors should be chosen on the basis of real intellectual interest rather than on the basis of vocational interests.

Your employer is guaranteed to be a paradox. (Did you learn that during interviews?) In all likelihood he won't care as much about what your major has been (he will ask, of course, he has to say something), as he will care about your personality. This fact has been emphasized throughout all the job descriptions given. Your knowledge of vocations is limited; everyone's is at the time academic choices must be made. When you have completed the work (as much as interests you) suggested in the preceding chapters, you will have a wider horizon, but that academic choice cannot wait.

6

SOMETHING CAN BE DONE ABOUT IT

> *To say that a feeling is unreal does not mean*
> *that we do not feel it, any more than to say that*
> *an idea is false means that we do not think it.*
> *An unreal or illusory emotion may be very*
> *strongly felt and it may influence our conduct*
> *profoundly. . . .*
> *There can be no hope of educating our emo-*
> *tions unless we are prepared to stop relying upon*
> *other people for our judgments of value. We*
> *must learn to feel for ourselves even if we make*
> *mistakes.*
>
> —JOHN MACMURRAY[1]

ONE OF THE LEADING BOOKS dealing with vocational problems says:

It is decidedly unfair to stimulate students to think of their
occupational future unless they have first been given an under-
standing of their own assets and liabilities. As a result of diagnosing
and counseling, students will be prevented from making unwise
choices which can lead only to failure and disappointment. . . . For
these reasons, therefore, individual diagnosis and treatment should
precede, or at least parallel *the dissemination of vocational infor-*
mation.[2]

The pattern of this handbook urges you to carry on the two
searches at the same time: the search for information about
the vocational world, and the search for an understanding of
yourself. In a winding path this workbook began with academic interests and proceeded to vocational information. The
subject of your quest for knowledge of your abilities ends the
book, but leads right back to the job you must do—of collect-

---

[1]Macmurray, John, *Reason and Emotion.* Appleton-Century-Crofts, Inc., New
York, 1943, pp. 33, 37.

[2]By permission from *Student Guidance Techniques,* by Donald G. Paterson,
Gwendolen G. Schneidler, Edmund G. Williamson. Copyrighted 1938 by
McGraw-Hill Book Co., Inc., New York, p. 271.

ing vocational information, checking yourself with your discoveries. You do the work and learn the lessons. Just as life is enriched by gathering vocational information during college, so, too, you should keep learning about your abilities as the four years pass. Having chosen college elective studies on the basis of intellectual interests, you have been gathering vocational information all the while; you must learn about your abilities and vocational interest concomitantly.

You do these things subconsciously anyway. If you don't have a plan for these activities while doing formal studying, you are just putting off these responsibilities until the final day when you must meet an employer, and will have to say something—fast.

aptitude tests can't do all the work

There are a number of pencil and paper tests which college counselors use to help bring to light your vocational interests, your personality traits and your abilities. Your college counselor knows that these tests show the "extent of a student's deviation from the average student,"[3] and whatever the score achieved on such tests, check with your own estimation of these personality traits. Few colleges have the resources to give many tests and to offer the counseling service which must interpret the results. The "Kuder Preference Record for College Women,"[4] if you have access to it, would be an interesting supplement to discoveries about your own preferences. Another test, the "Grace Mansion Occupational Interest Blank for Women," will rate you in relation to the group used for the experiment which validated this interest blank. Tests can be lifesavers. If you show yourself so little respect as to say: "I haven't the ghost of an idea what I want to do"; if you have been cloistered from the busy world to such a degree, then you will need tests to dig yourself out of oblivion. To be vocationally aware of yourself and of the only world you have to live in, is the plea of this workbook.

[3] *Op. cit.* p. 291.
[4] Kuder, G. Frederic, *Preference Record*, Science Research Associates, 1942.

No test has yet been devised which abolishes the responsibility for making a vocational choice—indeed, you would not wish to have the choice made *for you*. You are cheating yourself of half of the richness of liberal arts if you do not learn from Greek or Latin or any study in the curriculum, something about your own vocational abilities and aptitudes. As has been said repeatedly, the exercise of your active choice is an important part of your personal development. Whatever the circumstances, you can rightfully take pride in self-direction—take pride in saying, "It's up to me!"

You will not ask, then, of any course, "What job will this course or major prepare me for?" You will ask, "What is this study revealing to me about myself?" Human abilities have been divided into nine parts by one writer; into ten by another. To start you thinking about your own abilities, both of these are given:

Types of Human Abilities[5]

VERBAL: Ability to define, understand, and use words as symbols of meaning and experience.

NUMERICAL: Ability to manipulate (mentally) numbers as symbols of experience or meaning; to solve problems which involve numbers.

SPATIAL: Ability to think or solve problems (mentally) which present actual objects in space.

MEMORY: For detail.

DRILL: Routine memorizing of learning.

PHYSICAL AGILITY: Ability to coordinate large and small muscles; to manipulate objects with speed and precision.

MUSICAL: Ability to understand musical form and to perform on a musical instrument.

ARTISTIC: Ability to understand form, balance, color harmony and their use in artistic creation and interpretation.

---

[5]Williamson, E. G., *Students and Occupations*. Henry Holt, New York, 1937.

SOCIAL: Ability to work with people without friction; leadership.

THE SECOND LIST, GIVEN FOR EMPHASIS, IS SIMILAR.[6]

VERBAL AND LINGUISTIC: Fluency in use of one's own language and facility in learning other languages. Perception of verbal relations.

SCIENTIFIC: Facility in defining, classifying, grasping principles, inductive reasoning; perceiving relation of rule to example.

MATHEMATICAL: Facility with abstract symbols (and relations of cause and effect). Perception of complex number relations.

CLERICAL AND COMMERCIAL: Accuracy and speed in handling numbers, names, systems, and details.

CONSTRUCTIVE AND MECHANICAL: Perception of special relations. Facility in designing, calculating, working with machinery, etc.

MANUAL SKILLS: Dexterity in using tools with hands and fingers, precision in coordinating movements.

ARTISTIC: Appreciation of form and color; facility in crafts and in imaginative interpretations.

EXECUTIVE: Initiative, self-reliance, ambition, leadership, etc.

SOCIAL: Sociability, cooperativeness, tact, helpfulness.

PRACTICAL: Efficiency in practical affairs, calmness under pressure, persistence, courage.

All these abilities belong to all the studies: the sciences, biological and physical; the social sciences; the humanities, and to every job. At first glance, some abilities seem more closely allied to one study than another. For example, mathematical ability obviously belongs in the physical science but is not mathematical ability as defined in the second list also a part of

---

[6]*Ibid.*

each of the other three categories? And in what job is mathematical ability not useful? All knowledge is one.

The following pages provide the space for you to note in what ways your abilities are being defined by your studies.

Social Sciences

Name of course or courses:

Avocational interests in this field:

Name of skill mentioned on previous page or your own version.	What grade would you give yourself? If it's too high or too low, *time* will tell on you!	Why? Give examples.

What job titles do your abilities suggest?

Sciences

Name of course or courses:

Avocational interests in this field:

Name of skill.   What grade would   Why?
                      you give yourself?
_____   _____   _____

What job titles do your abilities suggest?

Humanities

Name of course or courses:

Avocational interests in this field:

Name of skill.	What grade would you give yourself?	Why?

What job titles do your abilities suggest?

ABILITY SUMMARY SHEET

On this and the next page, write a summary of the abilities inspection has brought to light. Be forthright. What abilities predominate? List them in order of the urgency you feel for their fulfillment. What ability brings you the greatest enjoyment in its use? This is the page (whatever it says) you might wish to bring to a counselor for further discussion, for testing, for defending or for corroboration. Put yourself on trial. In all justice to yourself, assume responsibility for being chief justice of your own supreme court. Hear the evidence, present your own defense, if necessary, and make the final decision. How wisely you decide will depend upon how well you understand yourself, how sincerely you have sought a vocational goal, how courageous you are in daring to face your true self.

Here you have begun to record a world of work as part of your first step. Here you have begun to record your abilities and your vocational assets. Here you have begun the discovery of the kingdom of heaven which is within you.

Summary—of YOU

1. What personality assets do I have? What liabilities?

2. Which special work abilities do I have?

3. What specific questions come to mind with regard to the next step I must take in relating my courses to a vocation? What help do I need to do this?

4. Am I using all the resources I now have—knowledge, finances, work experience—to the best of my ability?

ACKNOWLEDGMENTS

The author is indebted to the following individuals and companies who have supplied her with the information and suggestions used in the preparation of this manuscript. Their material appears on the pages indicated below.

Book-of-the-Month Club, personnel director, p. 27

American Airlines, Personnel Administration, pp. 30, 34, 98-100

New York Stock Exchange, pp. 30, 34, 38, 87

Street & Smith Publications Incorporated, pp. 32, 63-66

The Associated Press, Personnel Department, p. 32

National Broadcasting Company, Inc., employment manager, pp. 33, 36, 105

Burroughs Adding Machine Company, p. 38

Margaret M. Horn, Acme Fast Freight, Inc., p. 39

Mrs. Lea Cowles, assistant professor, specialist in Child Development, University of Alabama, pp. 46-47

Esso Standard Oil Company, pp. 51-52, 87

Time, Inc., pp. 52-53

Professor Camilla Low, associate professor of Education, University of Wisconsin, p. 53

Mrs. John McConnel, senior employment counselor, New York State Employment Service, pp. 53-54

The New York Times, personnel director, pp. 66-67

Cohn-Hall-Marx Company, Cohama Fabrics Division, p. 72

Memorial Hospital Center for Cancer and Allied Diseases, New York, personnel director, pp. 77-78

Mrs. Helen M. Miller, Miller Laboratory, and vocational counselor of the New York Chapter of the Registry of Medical Technologists, p. 80

Presbyterian Hospital in the City of New York, pp. 80-81

Louella E. Cable, aquatic biologist, U. S. Fish and Wildlife Services, pp. 84-85

American Institute of Public Opinion, pp. 87-88

Miss Elsie Bush, director of religious education, Faith Congregational Church, Springfield, Massachusetts, pp. 90-91

Mrs. Kathleen B. Stebbins, executive secretary, Special Libraries Association, p. 93

United Nations, director of personnel, pp. 95-96

The Metropolitan Museum of Art, Office of the Vice-Director, pp. 101-104

Metro-Goldwyn-Mayer, New York Office, p. 107

Twentieth Century-Fox Corporation, New York Office, personnel manager, p. 107

Mary E. Tetreault, Winfield Dress Company, Inc., p. 110

C. S. Hammond & Company, editor-in-chief, pp. 111-112

Silver Burdett Company Textbook Publishers, p. 114

INDEX

PRINTED IN THE UNITED STATES OF AMERICA
BY THE COMET PRESS, INC.
DESIGNED BY EDWIN B. KOLSBY